RUNWAYS
OF *My Life*

Adventures
OF A MILITARY AND CORPORATE PILOT

LEE SMITH

Print ISBN: 978-1-54398-594-8

PREFACE

In March of 1932, the Great Depression was coming to an end, the Lindbergh baby was kidnapped and murdered, Germany was preparing for war, and I began my life.

Birmingham, Alabama, was an interesting city to grow up in. There were steel mills, trains, and a good local park with an elephant called "Miss Fancy."

A few years later, as I grew, Germany invaded Poland and was threatening the rest of Europe. I was fascinated by the airplanes that took part in the conflicts. In my imagination, I was a fighter pilot with many kills to my credit. My favorite thing was to put a chair on the floor with the back down, on which I would sit, using the legs as my guns. I had many close calls, but was always victorious.

My grandmother wanted me to be a doctor like my grandfather, but also encouraged my talent as an artist.

Some of my ancestors fought in the Revolution and the Civil War (or "the War for Southern Independence") on the side of the Confederacy. Strange how every man who took part in the Revolution is considered a hero now, but not so the men of the Confederate states. In both wars, they fought for what they believed, and in both wars taxation and representation were an issue. Slavery was tolerated during the Revolution, but was an issue in 1861. Now, in 2018, the collective "National Conscience" has mandated the destruction of Confederate monuments and many more memories of the Old South, such as most of Stephen Foster's songs. Right or wrong, history is being rewritten. I find it a travesty, but I didn't pursue politics again until the war in Vietnam, in which I did participate. Anyway, I have an ancestor named Reed who died on the bridge at Concord, and several others who died at Shiloh and other battles. My own life almost ended in North Vietnam.

CHAPTER I

Growing Up

In 1939 our family moved to Marianna, Florida.

Due to having scarlet fever and rheumatic fever, I had a heart murmur and could not do athletics, so I joined the Marianna High School band. My earlier experiences playing the violin, which my aunt Bess taught me, helped my musical interests. Our band director, Herman Dean, had been a lead clarinet player in the John Philip Sousa band and was a strict disciplinarian. I advanced to lead trumpet player and was selected "Best Boy Musician," which may have been more of a popularity position than an award for a good musician, but I didn't turn it down. I did do some solos and enjoyed the experience. I'll always be grateful for the discipline I learned from Mr. Dean. That discipline helped me in my Air Force years and was essential to my survival and success. It is still important to me in everything I do. Other than my father, Mr. Dean was my childhood idol and hero.

Our move from Birmingham to Marianna was due to my father's changing from his job at his brother's scrapyard to a partnership in a limestone plant and farm equipment business. Marianna Limestone

Company dug limestone from a quarry, crushed it into powder, and spread it on fields around Jackson County. It improved the quality of the soil when it was too acidic. I got to drive one of the spreader trucks when I got older. That was thrilling to me, driving my own truck on a job! My older brother, Sam, was doing the same. The weather in northwest Florida changed to more rain during the year. This caused the limestone to get wet in the ground, making it impossible to crush into powder, so the limestone production slowed to a stop. The plant was abandoned and the truck sold. The farm equipment business was also slow, so my father sold his share to his partner and opened a business called Sam Smith Machinery. He bought WWII surplus equipment, cranes, trucks—anything and everything. I remember once when he acquired hundreds of oxygen masks from the Army Air Corps. Many had names or initials of aircrew members who had used them in the war. Some were new. He bought hundreds of fire extinguishers. I had the job of cleaning them for resale. During those days, my father started developing the fields around the old limestone plant and our house. At one time, we had seventeen hundred acres of land. I found myself driving mules; plowing; and carrying corn, peas, peanuts and whatever by mule-drawn wagons from our fields. Mules are smart. They know left and right: "gee" and "haw."

Growing up, I met many people. Many were black people, who had a most interesting and pleasant culture,—peaceful and spiritual. I can't remember a mean or spiteful one. One stands out in my mind as a fine and gentle person: Arthur Myrick. Arthur was an old man when I knew him. He would often drive up to our home near Marianna with his wife, two mules drawing their wagon. He would always remove his hat when he saw my mother and exchange pleasantries. Arthur did some work for my father when he was younger. When Arthur was a boy, he and his family had worked on the plantation where we now lived. They had been slaves.

The place we owned and built a house on about 1942 was once a plantation owned by Colonel Russ—the first name on the deed. He was a Civil War colonel, and he and his wife were buried in the field behind our house. We tried to preserve their limestone brick marker, which was about six feet long, three feet wide and four feet high. The graves had been ruined at some time by vandals, I guess. The bodies were no longer there. I found the remains of a slave graveyard; a few limestone markers were scattered in the woods not far from Col. Russ' grave. I remember the name "Liza" on one marker I found.

When not in school, I spent a lot of time hunting and fishing on our property. About a mile and a half from our house was a small creek that ran through the very thick woods and finally into the Chipola River. The Chipola ran into the Chattahoochee River, which flowed into the Gulf of Mexico.

My obsession for adventure drove me to attempt a trip down the creek to the Chipola River. My transportation was a home-built, eight-foot kayak, made of strips of wood covered with canvas. "Transportation" is a generous word for it, as I had to drag it a lot of the way over fallen trees and through the brush. I fished when I came to a good spot, catching a few small fish and seeing many cottonmouth snakes drop from trees into the creek near the boat. I spent most of the day doing this. At one point, I reached a deep spot where the creek was about twenty-five feet wide. Suddenly, a very large alligator arose from the weeds on the left bank, and with one quick motion, plunged into the creek less than ten feet from where I was. The wake from this monster rocked the kayak violently, but I stayed aboard, retracting my feet, which had been dangling in the cool water. No one ever said (until many years later) that I could walk on the water, but I truly wanted to do so then. Instead, I remained as still as I could, letting the kayak drift downstream above the deep place where I thought the gator had gone to the bottom.

About an hour or so later, as my nerves began to settle and my adrenaline stabilized, I caught a distinct sweet smell in the air. It was so out of place, it seemed odd until I realized I was graced with the odor of corn mash being cooked. I had just left one of the most dangerous killers in the swamp, only to stumble into the most dangerous thing in the swamp: a man with his liquorstill. I never caught sight of him, but he was there, all right, armed and ready to kill quickly to protect the secrecy of his operation. Well, if I was quiet as I drifted by the gator's spot, I breathed just enough to maintain consciousness as I put distance downstream between me and that sweet smell.

There is a very special peace and stillness when you are completely alone. No sound but the occasional bird chirping or squirrel calling. A sound is magnified against the otherwise total silence.

Even I'd had enough adventure for one day. Thankfully, the two or three hours to the Chipola were uneventful. The highway bridge over the Chipola looked fantastic. My calculations were correct, but it was pretty much guesswork, as I had no map and only someone's assurance that the creek ran to the river and the river ran under the highway. Ignorance is enhanced by stupidity, and I had my share of both. Finding a phone on the highway was challenging, although the details are long lost. I do remember my mother's shock and anger at what I had done, and that I then needed a ride home with the kayak. It was about twenty miles round trip from our house, which was west of Marianna, to the bridge, which was northeast of town.

Adventure was the thing that impressed me: the unknown, the unexpected, and the surprising. I was hooked—not on hunting (I don't enjoy killing), not on fishing (I get bored easily), but on the adventure. For hours at a time, Sam and I would explore the cave on our property. The big cave was about three-quarters of a mile in length, with many different chambers, beautiful formations, bats, and rattlesnakes.

Snakes were a part of life at "Redbud Ridge." We killed rattlesnakes thirteen feet long. My mother once shot a rattler near the back door with our 12-gauge shotgun. Redbud Ridge was beautiful with the redbuds and dogwoods in bloom, peaceful in the evenings, but deadly when the snakes were out. Dottye and I never really considered retiring there.

In 1950, I left for college. My brother, Sam, was already at the University of Alabama. We spent one year together at the university, both in the Sigma Alpha Epsilon fraternity.

CHAPTER 2

College Days

What were the things that I remember most from my time at the University of Alabama? Shamefully, not my academic record, which was unremarkable at best. I enrolled in art school and began a four-year party at a party school. To say the art department people were "fun-loving" folks doesn't give it the justice they deserve. "Dysfunctional" comes to mind when recalling the events, classes, gathering and outings of the art department. A typical event took place when we made home brew beer. We cooked it in the ceramics lab and got wasted consuming it in a traveling party, which no one could recall the ending to. There were some great guys in the fraternity, but I can't say that it added a lot to my character, much like the art department.

My dreams as a child of being a fighter pilot had long since seemed hopeless. But while at the university, the Air Force gave some of us an incentive flight in a T-33 jet trainer, which very much impressed me with its amazing performance, which rekindled my dream of flying, The fighter version of the T-33 was the F-80, the first jet that the US Air

Force (USAF) used in the Korean conflict, which was going on during my college days.

I became a squadron commander in the ROTC and stumbled through the rest of my classes to graduate with a Bachelor of Fine Arts degree and a commission as a second lieutenant in the USAF.

My conversion from art student to Air Force pilot was like changing a turkey into an eagle; a very different mindset was required. So my earlier lessons in discipline were about to pay off, profoundly. There were seven months between graduation and my assignment at pre-flight school at San Antonio, Texas, so I went to Miami and found a job as a parking attendant at the upscale Four Seasons Hotel at the Surf Club. I parked Cadillacs, Corvettes, Thunderbirds, and Rolls Royces, which was thrilling at my age of 24.

My Air Force days began with pre-flight school at Lackland Air Force Base in Texas. All I remember is a lot of physical training and crawling through the mud under barbed wire while some psycho fired a 50-caliber machine gun a few inches over my head. Wasn't this the flying branch of the service? It wasn't even called the Army Air Corps any longer. I did get lucky with an assignment to Primary Flight School in my hometown of Marianna, FL. It was a private contract school with civilian instructors. My instructor was Rusty Ost. He had a reputation as the toughest, but best instructor there. I recall getting violently airsick in a Piper Cub during my first three flights. I was not the sharpest student by far. I would at times forget to buckle the lap belt. This almost did me in when doing solo acrobatics. Once, a slow roll left me in a ball at the top of the cockpit against the canopy of a T-6 Texan. Since I was disconnected from the controls, I had to kick the control stick with my foot to roll the plane upright. Luckily I had the canopy closed, as that is what kept me inside. Timing is not only important, it can save your ass. A day or so before the incident with the T-6, I was doing slow rolls when I looked up (down toward the ground when inverted) to see the canopy was fully open—which was against the rules for good reason. Had the two mistakes occurred at the same time, well, you get the picture of me free falling from the T-6 above the Florida landscape. At any rate, by then I was hooked on flying and looking forward to the jets that I got to fly in basic flight school in Greenville, Mississippi. My first solo flight in the T-33 jet trainer was another step up the ecstasy ladder. I was the world's hottest pilot and really needed to do something outrageous, which turned out to be buzzing the University of Alabama campus at a very low altitude. It was wonderful, but it almost broke a basic rule of flying: wherever you go, be sure you have enough fuel to get back. After making it across two states to Greenville, my calculations of fuel remaining were less than optimistic, so I started conserving fuel. Oh yes, I was also lost. I was visual and knew I would eventually see the Mississippi River, but my fuel would be gone by then. But by that point, I would be in, as they say, "a very expensive glider." Call it luck or divine guidance, but I eventually spotted a reservoir called Grenada, which was shaped like an arrowhead. I took it for divine guidance and followed the direction of the arrow, which led me directly to Greenville. I landed with just enough kerosene to fill an oil lamp. I shudder to think what the consequences of that flight could have been.

Again, I wasn't the "Ace of the Base," but I received my pilot's wings and was assigned to a B-47 wing in Lake Charles, Louisiana. The B-47 was a six-engine jet, a strategic bomber designed by Boeing and used as a nuclear deterrent in the Cold War. We carried only one bomb, one big one. The aircraft had a crew of three: pilot, copilot, and navigator-bombardier. From 1956 to 1959, I was the copilot. My duties were to read checklists to the other two guys and fire the two twenty-millimeter cannons on the tail should an enemy fighter pilot be so foolish as to engage us in a tail chase. Oh yes, if something happened to the pilot, it was my duty to take over the controls and land the plane safely. What had happened to my dream of being a fighter pilot?

Lee in a T-33 jet trainer

Lake Charles was important because it is where I met Dottye Tate, a schoolteacher and the one love of my life. Our first encounters were rather awkward. I was certainly not a great catch, a scruffy B-47 copilot who often would hang out with a group much like me, with a keg of beer in the back of a station wagon. I was doing some painting at that time and was never what you would call presentable when off duty. A mutual friend introduced Dottye and me, but it didn't work out. During the next year, we saw each other at parties we both happened to be at. Eventually, we did go out together. We started to talk about what we each would like for a wedding; oddly, we wanted nearly the same details. As it turned out, we were planning our wedding. But, she was interested in one of the tanker pilots. I did not look down on tanker pilots, but felt that they provided a service, something like a gas station, where the B-47 could refuel while airborne. The aircrews of the B-47 were away from home a lot, whether on strip alert on base or on temporary assignments to bases in the North or to England, where we slept near the aircraft and the big nuclear weapon in the bomb bay. Oceanic navigation in the '50s was done using celestial navigation, a system that used the stars, such as Sirius and Arcturus, and declination tables to compute your position. For this system, you had to use a sextant, which you could insert in a port in the canopy to average the angle of the star as the aircraft pitched and rolled in the sky. A thirty-mile error was considered dead on. Of course, the UK and Europe are big, and you are bound to find something eventually.

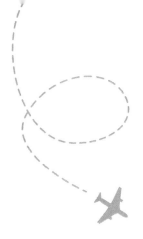

CHAPTER 3

Dottye

I was a lousy copilot. Looking back on it, I was more interested in my love life, but I had to deal with the tanker pilot, who was showering Dottye with gifts he brought back from his trips overseas. He even proposed, leaving her a ring and waiting for an answer. That was it! I had had enough. I cornered Dottye one day and proposed. To my surprise, she said yes.

We decided on a January wedding. About six hundred people were to come to the Baton Rouge church. But I was on a of the two-week assignment in Maine. We were scheduled to fly back to Lake Charles two days before the wedding. It was snowing in Maine; the base closed because the weather was too bad for flying except for an operational launch if the bell rang. Finally, our flight was released. But we had a problem: our B-47 needed an engine change. The beast had six GE engines, and believe me, it required all six running to get it off the ground. I recall being there, in the snow, while the mechanics changed the engine. I believed they understood my panic, and time was running out. One of the mechanics cut himself, and drops of blood landed in the snow beneath the number 4 engine. They finished the job, and the next morning we were taking the icy runway when the nose wheel lost traction. We started to slide across the ice toward the runway edge. It would have been the end of the flight, but Chelsey, the captain, was able to correct it and realign on the runway, then take off. The landing gear retraction was not successful, and it showed an unsafe condition. Chelsey said that we should return and land according to the rules, at which point I said we would have a problem putting the landing gear handle down, as there would be a size 12 boot below it, preventing the extension. So we all agreed to continue to Lake Charles Air Force Base (AFB). However, I was required to get out of my parachute and crawl through a tiny crawlway, which passed the nose landing gear on the way to the bomb bay. Through a peephole, I could read "BF Goodrich" on the tire, which confirmed it was in the gear well. My friend, Lieutenant Manning was waiting on the ramp, and we stopped next to his Oldsmobile convertible. I threw my B-4 bag in the back and jumped in for the one and a half-hour trip to Baton Rouge, where the wedding was to be the next morning. Ray Tate, my future father-in-law, was on the edge of hysteria when it appeared that I was snowed in at the base in Limestone, Maine. He was about to call General Curt LeMay, chief of strategic air command. It was my good luck he didn't find the right number. I think he did reach Russell Long, the Louisiana senator, who advised him not to call the general. My parents had arrived the day before and were all sitting around staring at Dottye's folks; a really awkward time, I'm told. Anyway, the wedding went off as planned.

I thought that I had recovered from all the stress of getting to the wedding, but I may have been hallucinating as Dottye came down the aisle on her dad's arm. With the veil covering her face, I did not recognize her and I started to wonder if her parents had switched her with an unknown crazy sister or cousin. I was in such shock that I would still go through with it! But as the veil was raised, Dottye's face was revealed, and I gave a profound sigh of relief.

On our honeymoon trip, we got as far as Orange, Texas, near the Louisiana state line. We thought we were playing it cool as I registered at the front desk. But about then, Dottye pulled her hand out of her fur muff (the style in 1958), and a lot of rice fell to the marble floor. It sounded like hail and lasted for about thirty seconds. Laughter and knowing looks confirmed everyone there was aware we were newly-weds. Our destination was Laredo, Mexico, but I ran short of money when we reached Corpus Christi, so that was our honeymoon stop.

Months later, when Dottye was pregnant, we moved into our first house. One night, while we were sleeping, I had the most vivid dream that I was in the basement of the Delta Gamma sorority house at the University of Alabama. I had never actually been there, but I was trapped and couldn't get out. My way was blocked by a solid mass of butterscotch pie. No crust, just butterscotch. I began to scoop it up, digging my way out with handfuls of butterscotch, not making much progress, when a bee landed on my hand. Not wanting to be stung, I swung my hand against something to knock it off. When I woke up, I found I had just hit Dottye with the back of my hand. I tried to tell her about my dream but could not explain how I came to be under the Delta Gamma house.

Our little house on Meadow Drive cost less than $15,000, but it was a lot of money for a second lieutenant in 1958. We rented it to a family from 1960 to about 1962 when I was reassigned to another base That was a miserable experience. The tenants paid the rent two months late—if they paid at all—damaged the house, and finally left without giving notice. Unfortunately, the base was closing and real estate values plummeted. We finally had to just walk away, leaving the house with the bank.

In 1960, we went to Maxwell Air Force Base in Montgomery, Alabama, for about three months. There, I attended Squadron Officer School, where the junior officers were trained in leadership and air warfare tactics.

The course was organized into small groups of about eight or nine officers, who were given air tactical problems and situations. We were also each given subjects to develop and give a demonstration to the class. One project was of my own choosing. I maintained that if the weather could be controlled, a nation could gain tactical advantage. Cloud seeding was in the experimental stage, primarily for agricultural purposes. I proposed that if we could change the weather, we might change the outcome of a battle. The instructor considered the idea preposterous. Today, we know it is a real possibility. Another of my ideas that did not align with the "school solution" was the idea of limited wars. 1960 was in the Cold War era, and de Seversky's book, *Air Power: Key to Survival* was practically the Air Force's bible. The next war would be the big one, complete with nukes. I believed that opposing nations would use their nuclear arsenals as their "ace in the hole," while knowing full well the other nation would not risk global war to counter a small conflict of force or seizure of territory. The result would be a "limited" war, where all civilized nations would not allow the unthinkable to happen. The idea of limited war was certainly not in Alexander P. de Seversky's book. So again, I did not follow the school's thinking (or non-thinking). Now, in 2018, we know we've had nothing but limited wars and conflicts for years. Our group, I think, had the only female offi-cer and the only black officer in the course. The instructor was fond of those who played "flickerball" for our group. They were considered the "neat guys." The woman, the black man, and I were in the "slob" group and proud of it. Somehow, we got into a discussion about polar bears, and the fact that they often hunt with a paw over their black noses. It occurred to me that their identities could be further concealed if they also wore dark sunglasses. This absurd idea delighted the group, at least the "slobs," and it became a thing of great amusement toward the end of the course. I found it somewhat of a relief from my frustration, concluding that this also was not the "school solution."

Next, Dottye and I went to Keesler AFB, in Biloxi, Mississippi, where I attended an electronics course to qualify as a communica-tions-radar officer. My great fear growing up was math. I disliked it at every turn. During my four years in college, I never put math in my world—art school, what can I say? But there I was at electronics school, my days packed with math challenges. So, I gave it all I had and finished the one-year course, tying for first in the class with an electrical engineer graduate. My greatest fear had become my great success.

My first assignment was an accompanied tour (I could take the family) to the Philippines. Dottye was pregnant with our son Chip at the time, so I was able to beg out of that assignment. Next was a manda-tory, remote (no family) tour in Iceland for a year. I went, but brought Dottye and our two kids, at my expense, to Iceland, where we found an upstairs apartment in the fishing village of Keflavik. Dottye had the very challenging job of flying to Iceland with two kids, one of whom had to be carried most of the time. Adding to this, Chip, the baby, was prone to scream when not perfectly comfortable. If that wasn't enough, the flight was on Friday the 13th, and their seats were 13A and 13B.

Of course, I was confused about their arrival time in Reykjavik and arrived at the airport late. By the time I arrived at the terminal, everyone had heard enough of the screaming child and knew the story of the late-to-arrive husband and father. So, as I opened the door to the small terminal lounge, I was met by a standing ovation—mostly, I think because the other passengers realized the screamer would soon be gone. Soon, we arrived at our apartment in Keflavik. The landlady, a rather unpleasant little person, was a known communist who asked for US dollars as rent payment. It was illegal to do this, so I refused and paid with Icelandic króna, which made her even more unpleasant. The apartment was always cold, with ice on the inside of the windows. At the time, there were no refrigerators in Iceland, so we hung the few perishables we had by a string on the outside of a window. But more than once, the wind would cause the string to break, sending the refrigerated items to the ground below, where the waiting sheep would feast. One day, an Icelandic man came to the door and told Dottye that "they" knew who we were and about our situation with the communist woman. The local people wanted us to know that most Icelanders were not like that. He said he would take us to another place, where the people were kind. This is when we met Hanna, whose mother owned the house we were to rent, Hanna remained our very good friend for the next forty years.

Life in Keflavik was not always easy—OK, it was never easy! Anything except Icelandic lamb and fish was subject to a high import tax, and therefore was very expensive. You could find anything on the US naval base, but you were forbidden to take any of it off the base due to the raging black market in Iceland. Many people made a nice living selling cigarettes smuggled from the base. We invented many ways to "smuggle" things from the base commissary and Base Exchange. We had our car, a 1957 Chrysler, shipped from the states. It had these beautiful big tail fins, which were hollow. I would tie several jars of baby food on the end of a long string, practically undetectable when the trunk was open, safely hidden inside the tail fins. The Marines and Icelandic guards were thorough in their car inspections, even removing door panels to expose cigarettes or other things stored there, but they never found our baby food stash.

The Air Force had only a small contingent in Iceland, centered at Rockville Air Station, a radar and long-range communications site, plus three other radar sites around the coast. Winters at Rockville were brutal. Ropes were strung between the buildings so men could go from one to the other safely in the driving snow. It wasn't unusual to see an aircraft blown off the runway or taxiway. I was once blown off a taxiway in a T-33 jet trainer with the brakes set!

I got my monthly flight time by flying a T-Bird and dragging a small target on the end of a long cable. The local Air Force pilots, in F-89 Scorpions, would shoot rockets at the target I towed. I never felt very comfortable with this, knowing the accuracy record of the 2.75-inch diameter "Mighty Mouse" rockets. The fighter pilots were a wild bunch who would party at a moment's notice and pick fights with the Navy "finks" at the club.

The fighter pilots' club was one room in the officers' quarters on base. I remember during one wild fighter party, the guys had a go-cart they were racing up and down the hallway. A young, indignant Navy ensign would viciously slash at the tires with his parade sabre. This encounter only caused the intensity of the challenge of the go-cart race to increase. I don't know the outcome of that fracas, but I do know that defeat was not a fighter pilot's option.

It was well known that nothing was sacred to the fighter gang, but they did show a certain brand of respect. One of them, the oldest, whom they called "Gray Squirrel," became unstable (even by their standards) and was found hiding behind a door holding a knife. He was sent back home to the States. After he was gone, the gang flew a "missing ship" formation in his honor. That's when you have a four-plane formation, and one leaves the group in flight, representing the one who was lost. It was thereafter known as "Gray Squirrel's missing ship formation." The fighter pilots demonstrated their feelings about the Navy and the admiral in general, by flying low over his quarters every Friday with a flight of four, lighting their afterburners as they passed over. Eight afterburners activated together make an uncommonly loud sound and strong shockwave that will penetrate a concrete bunker. This routinely brought the squadron commander before the admiral to explain the performance.

The last stunt I remember was the day the pilots lowered the admiral's flag from the pole in front of headquarters and raised a pair of pink panties to replace it. It was midafternoon before anyone noticed it, causing a huge commotion to get it all back to normal again.

One fond memory of our year in Iceland was a trip to Akureyri with Hanna. Her parents had a farm near there, which was within the Arctic Circle. We made the trip in a Douglas DC-3—which had an interior that was spartan at best, bucket seats and all—courtesy of Flugfélag, an Icelandic airline. The Akureyri airport was very basic as well, with a gravel runway. But the visit to the farm was outstanding. Hanna's father had Icelandic ponies, which Carol, our oldest and Chip had a great time riding, and a swimming pool in their barn. They were very cordial and treated us well.

We took two trips on the admiral's airplane. One was to London, which became our favorite city. We saw *The Music Man* with Van Johnson, whom we got to meet at the stage door—unusual for us, as we never waited for anyone at a stage door or wanted autographs. Mr. Johnson was very nice and surprised that we came from Iceland. Since seeing that musical, our song has been "Till There Was You."

We made a trip to Frankfurt on the admiral's Lockheed Constellation which had space available for military families. That turned out to be a longer trip. We rented a car in Frankfurt and drove all around Western Europe, stopping when and where we felt like it. The first stop was at Rüdesheim am Rhein, Germany, where they were having a wine festival. It was a charming old town surrounded by vine-yards, where crowds had gathered to drink the new wine. The taverns would hang a pine branch outside as a sign of the new wine being served. We finally settled into one with an oom-pah band and wild dancing. The locals were there as well, and very friendly to us even though we could not speak German. I don't remember how the wine was, though I consumed at least my share and kept buying drinks for the band. I vaguely remember walking back to our hotel with the band members in tow, laughing at anything and everything. Approaching the desk clerk, I asked in English for the key to room 242. He shook his head repeatedly as I kept asking and finally he pointed to the board, which held all the hotel's keys. There were places for about ten keys, and he suggested that we probably wanted the one for room number seven. The next day was not so good. The "new" wine was beginning to punish me mercilessly. Sunglasses helped the situation, plus it rained steadily all day. I have great memories of Bavaria, King Ludwig castles and other wonderful places in Bavaria. 1961 and 1962 were good times to be in Europe. The countries were recovering rapidly after the war, it was peaceful and everything was pretty relaxed. We left Bavaria after a few days and stopped at a guesthouse in Belgium . The proprietor there acted like he might have been a Nazi, or at least a collaborator, and made us a little uncomfortable. Otherwise, roaming around Europe in a rental car was a magical experience.

CHAPTER 4

California

We left Iceland in 1962, as I was reassigned as a communications and electronics officer at a NORAD radar station near Red Bluff, California. It is a small town in northern California that had an annual festival called the "Bull Shippers Convention." Nothing particularly remarkable happened at Red Bluff, other than my near-death experience, which occurred during a parade at the Bull Shipper's Convention. I was inside of a dragon float, operating its tail and eyes and sending smoke through the mouth. The dragon was mounted on a truck, and the truck's exhaust was right below me. After about an hour, I started to lose the use of my arms and legs. Then my sight failed, but I still could hear very well. The girls riding on the float kept calling to me to make the dragon do this and do that, but I could do nothing. Finally the parade ended and everyone left, except for two or three guys whom I could hear talking. Fortunately, one said, "Did that guy ever get out of the dragon?" The other said he didn't know, at which point they dragged me out by my feet and tried to revive me, assuming I was drunk and had passed out. It took a few days to recover, and as many to convince them I had carbon monoxide poisoning and nearly died.

During my assignment at the Red Bluff radar station, I had an additional duty as UFO officer—as in unidentified flying objects. I was to collect any information that came to the site regarding UFOs. The radar site was located at the eastern edge of the Trinity Alps; much of the area had not been well surveyed and charted. Many strange things happened there and people had disappeared in the very rough terrain. I don't remember all of the reports of UFOs, but one stands out as really weird. A young man riding bareback on a mule appeared one day with a strange story to tell. It seems he was walking in the mountains when he came upon an old truck abandoned by the roadside. As he approached, he could hear a scratching sound that seemed to come from the inside of the truck bed. When he reached a point a few feet away, he saw, quite clearly, a hand and part of an arm was scratching on the floor of the truck. Nothing was attached to the arm, but it continued to move. He became frightened and ran away. He never returned to that place, but felt he had to report this unusual thing. Such things as this were a challenge to reality, of course, but I was required to report this as my duty, even though there was no "flying object" involved. There were a number of other sightings that did involve "flying objects." The usual lights would appear and move in the sky, some at the wish or command of the observer. But somehow, the guy with the mule was different. Bigfoot's home territory was supposedly the Trinity hills, with numerous sightings reports, but in none was he seen flying. About fifty miles east of the radar site and controlled by my radar crew was a "gap filler" radar, which was positioned high on a mountain peak to fill a gap in our main radar coverage. It sustained itself with its own generators and sent radar returns to the Red Bluff station. Some of the men who had gone to the gap filler site to resupply it claimed to have seen Bigfoot. In their stories he was in a rage, lifting fifty-five-gallon drums and throwing them across the yard. True? I can't say.

By 1963, the Air Force notified me that I should accumulate at least seven years as a pilot as primary duty. More than ready to leave the C&E world and return to flying, I requested that they assign me to an aircraft with one seat and one engine. I'd had my fill of the Strategic Air Command, six-engine B-47s, and six- to eight-hour missions.

Surprisingly, the Air Force accommodated me by offering me a one-seat, one-engine F-102 Delta Dagger. My dream had arrived!

The high point of the F-102 training at Perrin AFB in Texas was the birth of our third child, David. But there, I got the first taste of what being a fighter pilot was really like: an indescribable rush of power and freedom. You think everyone should experience the feeling, and yet you want it all to yourself. You could spend a lifetime in a multiengine aircraft and not have one minute of the experience a fighter pilot has while airborne.

It was a quiet time at Perrin, other than my transition to fighter pilot. I did have a friendly fight with my next-door neighbor, who didn't share my political views. We played tricks on each other with bumper stickers and such. But the best came when I put my initials in his front lawn with fertilizer. I then watered the grass each night. It took some time, but the big letters could be seen from at least half a block away. The display remained for weeks, as he could do nothing to remove it.

After qualifying as an F-102 fighter pilot, I was assigned to an interceptor squadron at Seymour Johnson AFB in Goldsboro, North Carolina. The 482nd Squadron was composed of a group of F-102 jocks, all a bit touched in the head and each knowing he was the world's best fighter pilot. I was living my dream: a one-seat, one-pipe, delta-wing fighter.

Four of us at the time were deployed to Key West Naval Air Station in Florida to sit on strip alert next to the runway. We would respond to any aircraft off track or MIGs that would venture close to or in our airspace. Once, the bell rang before dawn indicating an unidentified aircraft. I jumped out of the bunk, where I slept fully clothed, and ran to the aircraft with another pilot, who ran to his aircraft. The crew chief helped me strap in as I started the engine and pushed the throttle forward. I was leading, and the runway was only about a hundred feet ahead. Less than one minute after the bell rang, we lit the afterburners and started the takeoff roll. I've heard of people sleepwalking, and I don't know if I did that day, but I suddenly realized there was only a very black sky in front of me and the glow of instruments in the cockpit. I was very awake after that, until "Blackstone" radar, the intercept control, vectored us close to the target. It was a Nicaraguan Airlines plane, an old DC-3–type aircraft with a top speed about equal to our stall speed. That meant that we had to lower the landing gear, slow to almost stall speed, and sweep the landing light across the target's tail to get the number. With all that, I had to be really close to him to read the numbers as I passed. Only then could we identify the target, which was off the airway a few miles. We would fly the planes back to North Carolina after a two week stay at Key West, carrying a big sack of Florida lobsters in lobster season in the missile bay. While at Seymour Johnson, another captain and I were temporarily assigned to Myrtle Beach, South Carolina, to take part in the testing of procedures for the Strategic Arms Limitation Treaty (SALT). This involved inspection procedures mostly and took two or three months. During that time, the squadron closed due to the aircraft being obsolete. But they didn't advise us, so we came back to a base with no fighter squadron. I called headquarters at Washington Air Defense Sector. They did not know about us, but after checking, said we would be called Detachment 2 of the Washington Air Defense Sector. There was no assigned duty or work. I was commander of a detachment with only one other officer assigned to it. Every month, we would switch as commander. Eventually, I was assigned to an F-102 squadron in Hahn, Germany, but that fell through because the F-102 had become obsolete and the Air Force closed all of the units. The F-102s went to the Air National Guard. I was reassigned to an RF-4C Phantom, a reconnaissance aircraft. My new base was the original escadrille WWI base at Toul-Rosières, in France, where they flew SPADs and Nieuports. The same insignia they had used during WWI was on the new Phantoms of the 22nd Tactical Reconnaissance Squadron, which I became part of.

Lee and the F-102

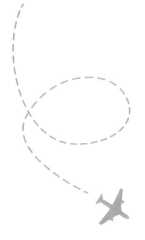

CHAPTER 5

Europe

I was in France a few months before we got base housing and Dottye came over with the kids — Carol, Chip, and David. Flying around Europe was great in the '60s, as there were almost no restrictions and little traffic.

At first, we lived in base housing at the Toul-Rosières Air Base. It was comfortable, but not fancy. We got to know some of the other base-housing families. One couple kept an ocelot in their bathroom. It slept in the tub at night and escaped on more than one occasion, causing more than a little panic. Dottye and I took a trip to Paris with another couple. Our stay in Paris was highlighted by one our fondest memories: a river trip on the Seine on a Bateaux Mouche. It was a dinner cruise, during which we watched slack-rope walkers along the banks of the Seine. An opera group was also on board, having dinner. They sang for much of the time we were there; very impressive. The group seemed to enjoy performing for us.

While returning to the base the next day, we were following a Citroën with a French family inside, when it struck an oncoming car.

The Citroën flipped over and came to rest upside down in a ditch beside the road. We stopped to help, finding several people in the car, most with injuries. Our friend, who was with us, spoke French and asked one of them if she had children. Hearing this, the woman screamed, saying her baby was missing. We found the child under the car; she had a bad head injury. When the ambulance arrived 2 hours later, Dottye was asked to ride with them and hold the child. We had to leave before finding out how the child did after getting to the hospital.

I got involved in flying new Phantoms from the factory in St. Louis to the base in France. During the first six-ship formation's flight over, my rudder suddenly started to vibrate violently. I slid out of the tight-knit formation to check it out, but it continued. Since we were close to Bermuda, our abort base, I landed at Kingsley Field to get repairs. After some inspections , test flights, several excursions in the base sailboat, and snorkeling for lobsters, we gave up and I flew the bird to Georgia for maintenance. During the next delivery flight, my wing-man was unable to air-refuel. The receptacle did not open, so we both landed in Bermuda. Again, it was another "hardship" delay in paradise, with sun, fun, and sailing. I don't recall why I had to land the third time in Bermuda, but I do recall that as I established on final approach, the tower operator asked, "Would you be Captain Smith?" I must have held the record for transient aircraft visiting repeatedly. All of this time, Dottye and the three kids were in a housing development close to the base. The only phone belonged to the landlord, a not-so-pleas-ant Frenchman named Mr. BonAmi. Mr. BonAmi came to our house to find Dottye, saying, "I am not a telephone" in broken English. After repeating this, he said, "Your husband fly up, and he go down. I am not a telephone!" Then he left. After some frantic inquiries, Dottye found out what was happening through friends from the base.

Eighteen months after I arrived at Toul-Rosières, President de Gaulle had all American bases closed, so we ferried all the planes to Mountain Home AFB in Idaho. This was our new home and my final base before leaving the Air Force. During this time, I volunteered to go to Vietnam along with eight other pilots and navigators. Five of the nine came back.

I stopped at Clark AFB in the Philippines to go through jungle survival school, but it was monsoon season and the class before mine had lost seven men in mudslides caused by the rain. Our jungle experience was cancelled, and we went to our base, Tan Son Nhut Air Base, near Saigon. We stayed at a small compound downtown, guarded by Chinese mercenaries. The food was decent and the air was damp and hot. The flights were short and simple. The Air Force did not allow personal weapons and issued short-barrel .38s to pilots. But I had bought a nice 9-millimeter semi-automatic before leaving Idaho and was determined to keep it with me. I had bought some carved wooden fruit (bananas, apples, et cetera) at the Clark Base Exchange. Since I had a leather case for the gun, I packed it full of the wooden fruit as a decoy, locked it, and gave it to the sergeant in charge of firearms. The case did appear to have the gun inside, and I think the sergeant believed it; therefore the "exchange" took place. I kept my 9-millimeter in a shoulder holster for the duration of my deployment in Vietnam.

We lost some aircraft and crews in Thailand while I was in Saigon, so I and others were reassigned to Udorn Royal Thai Air Force Base in Thailand. It was near Vientiane, Laos, on the Mekong River. From there we could easily fly over North Vietnam and Laos. Our missions were reconnaissance. We would gather intelligence about enemy activity as well as bomb damage assessment. The Phantom was equipped with several special cameras, both infrared and radar. A few minutes after the smoke would clear after a bombing attack, we would fly over the target to get bomb damage assessments. Other missions were to track enemy activity.

During my time off in Thailand, I would occasionally find things to draw. The Buddhist temples were good subjects. It was sometimes a distraction when a few monks gathered around to see what this crazy American was doing. I also did a drawing of Monique, our Laotian cleaning girl. When the cleaning girls took a break for lunch, they would form a circle, squat, and claw at the soft ground until they retrieved several creatures such as lizards and worms from beneath the surface. No cooking was involved, but they consumed everything. We were grateful for the good food at the officer's club.

The club was also a place to release your emotions on occasion. "Inappropriate" was not a term often used there. I remember a lieutenant colonel making a "carrier landing." To do this, the tables were placed end to end for about thirty feet, I guess. Then they lifted the colonel up onto one end of the tables and sent him sliding on his belly, headfirst, to the other end. I don't think naval officers would see the humor in our version of carrier landings.

I well remember August 12, 1967, when we were to fly over Hanoi after a strike to destroy a railroad bridge. I don't know how many of our F-105s were lost, but I do know that the information about the strike, like all strikes, was given in advance to the North Vietnamese by our Secretary of State, Dean Rusk. The North Vietnamese were again prepared and ready to defend. After turning south over "Thud Ridge" (named after the many F-105s that are still there), my wingman, Ed

Atterberry, was hit by an SA-2 missile. Ed and his backseater, Tom Parrott, were able to eject, but were captured and spent time in the "Hanoi Hilton." Ed escaped from the POW camp three times, but was killed by his captors after the third attempt. Tom was repatriated years later. My aircraft was not hit, and we continued to the target to get the images. I have no idea how many surface-to-air missiles (SAMs) they sent up after us, but our launch receivers indicated a missile was being guided almost continuously. After passing over the target, I jinked the RF-4C rather violently to confuse the missiles, losing track of time until I realized I was doing Mach 1.8 over "Banana Valley," a relatively safe area south of north Vietnam. I was very low on fuel. The Phantom has twelve minutes of fuel from full (no external tanks) to empty when using full afterburners. I called for a tanker, but was able to make it to Udorn without refueling, so I canceled the tanker. That day resulted in a Silver Star for me and my navigator, Frank Doyle, though I doubt it was well deserved. It was routine to have all cameras and sensors operating during the flight when approaching or over the target, so when my wingman was hit by the missile, my camera captured the whole sequence. These photos were on display in the Smithsonian Air and Space Museum for some time.

We lost some fine pilots over there. Many were lost through the actions of our own government, which shared target information with the North Vietnamese with the excuse of reducing collateral damage. There is a right way to fight a war, but that wasn't it.

I went to Bangkok and the Philippines on rest and recuperation during my months in Thailand. Pattaya Beach was a good place to find peace and total quiet. I called Dottye to say I was OK after the bad day over Hanoi. Tom Parrott's house was just down the street from ours at Mountain Home AFB, so Dottye went to see Tom's wife, thinking that she had heard about the situation—but Dottye quickly realized she had not. Shortly after Dottye got there, the base Chaplain was at the door of the Parrotts' home. It was a good thing that Dottye was there, as Tom's wife would have been alone when the Chaplain left.

I finished my tour and went back to Mountain Home, feeling very fortunate to have survived, yet somehow guilty that I did.

I somehow got lucky and landed the best pilot job on base. I was the test pilot for the reconnaissance wing at Mountain Home AFB. All aircraft went through twelve phases of maintenance inspections. When the twelfth check was completed, a thorough systems inspection is done and the engines were reinstalled, they gave the aircraft to me to test fly before putting it back in service. I checked all systems and flight control responses, then flew it to about 50,000 feet. There, I would accelerate to Mach 2, which is twice the speed of sound. Only one aircraft, a Phantom, would not reach Mach 2. At Mach 1.9, there was a compressor stall in the left engine. It sounded like a shotgun being fired by my left ear. The Phantom lurched sharply, with the tail rising as if it might tumble forward—not what you would like at that speed. But it recovered to normal, including the engine. I returned the plane to maintenance, suggesting they recheck the engine. They did, but found nothing. They gave it to me again for another test flight, which I did with exactly the same experience. They had to find out what was going on. My luck had been stretched to the limit. This time they did find the problem: The left engine, when reinstalled, did not seat correctly. This disrupted the airflow through the engine inlet at very high airspeed, hence the compressor stall – the compressor blades can't handle the amount of air flowing through the engine.

While stationed at Mountain Home, we made frequent visits to Fritchman Galleries in nearby Boise. Fritchman displayed some of my paintings which I had done during free time from the Air Force. We became friends with the Fritchmans, who were kind enough to train me in the art of framing. This was useful for my own works, but I planned to use the skill if I ever bought an art supply store which was a possibility after I left the Air Force. We made a trip to Napa, California, to look at a shop for sale. We did check it out but with no retail experience and little money, we did not think it would work, so we just had a nice tour of the wine country. I even investigated an art shop near Daytona, Florida, but that didn't work out either. So, I concluded that the art world might not be the answer. The art supply shop was not a good solution. Better that I try to pursue my other skill: aviation.

To be a good fighter pilot, you have to believe you're the best in the world, and I was convinced I was. But I'm really not a true warrior and lack the "killing" instinct. So, for many reasons, in 1968, I decided to leave the Air Force.

Certificate for Hanoi fotos

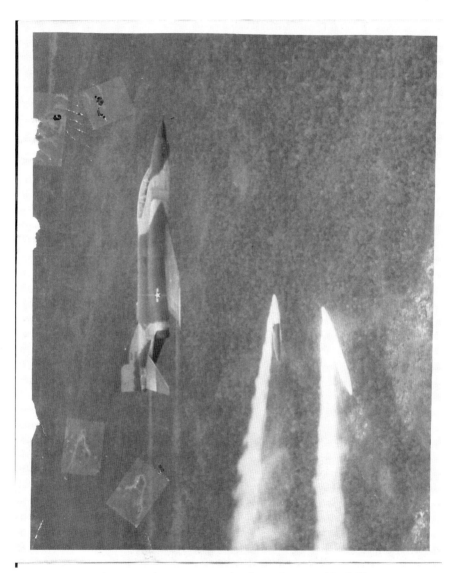

RF-4C Phantom II dropping external tanks on the way to North Vietnam

CHAPTER 6

A Civilian Again

A visit to the Boise Cascade flight department revealed the world of corporate aviation. I remember how tiny the Learjet 24 was and how small the controls and switches were compared to what I was used to. The proper way to land a Phantom is to slam it onto the runway, the same as on carrier landings. My interviewer introduced a rather different concept: being so gentle with the flight controls that the passengers would forget they were flying and the landings became a tender kiss when contacting the runway. I had quite a transition ahead of me.

The transition was not made easier by the first Learjet captain I was paired with, a wife-beater and a bully in the cockpit as well. My employer was Danny Schwartz, president of Pacifiic Cascade Land Corporation, a nice enough guy, with about $25 million in assets—pretty good in 1968 dollars. Later, he did well as the CEO of Bantam Books. His wife, Natalie, was somewhat eccentric at the age of about 48. She had a habit of stopping her chauffeur to pick up stray cats.

On one occasion, I was flying Danny's Learjet out of Palm Springs; we were taking Jimmy Van Heusen, the song and musical writer, somewhere. Dottye happened to be with us on that trip (Danny was very generous about that). Jimmy asked Dottye to hold his two small dogs while he sang some excerpts from *Thoroughly Modern Millie* that he had written. Danny's dream was to meet and become friends with Frank Sinatra. Within a year, through mutual friends, Danny did become a good friend of Frank Sinatra's. In the process, I got to meet him when he was our passenger.

Danny and Natalie moved to Cathedral City, outside of Palm Springs, California, and built a rather large house on the Tamarisk Golf Course down the fairway from good ol' Frank. His new home became known as "Fort Surprise," because it look like a fortress and had what looked like a moat around it. I was able to visit Ft. Surprise a few times, usually to do something for Natalie. She had the idea that since I was a pilot, I might have many talents. One task was to set the time on her new barometric clock, which no one else at Ft. Surprise could do. I knew as much about barometric clocks as I did about astrophysics, which was zero, but I piddled around with it until it ran the correct time. That did it. Twice a year, I went to Ft. Surprise to set that blasted clock! Once, Natalie called me when she discovered the large ceramic elephant she'd had shipped from Gump's in San Francisco was in a thousand pieces. I had to restore it; another perfect pilot job. I managed another minor miracle and Natalie was charmed. We flew Frank and Danny to Las Vegas, where they got lucky at Baccarat. They returned to Palm Springs on the Lear with $1 million in cash. I got to see a lot of $100 bills, but none were mine, save the occasional tip.

One Christmas, the captain (the wife abuser) and I each got a call to come to Ft. Surprise and bring our wives. We pilots were presented with special clocks (not barometric) "so we wouldn't be late," and our wives were each given five hundred-dollar bills. They were totally shocked. That was a nice Christmas.

The first encounter I had with Mr. Sinatra was when he got on the Learjet for a trip to Las Vegas. He was very cordial, but I did not expect him to remember me at all; why would he? The next evening at Caesar's Palace, where we always stayed, Mr. S was in line in front of me at the coffee shop. He turned and said, "Hi Lee!" I was so stunned, I could hardly reply. He was never anything but nice and friendly with us. He was somewhat less cordial with journalists and press folks. The flight crew was always expected to go backstage when Mr. S. performed; they sometimes chatted with the other pilot and myself outside the dressing room. Our wives were sometimes flown to Las Vegas on a chartered aircraft from Palm Springs. Once, they had to return to Palm Springs by commercial flight, and take some of Danny and Natalie's luggage. Their luggage turned out to be many fancy bags, which raised the eyebrows of the others in the baggage check line. So the women thought they would have some fun and started talking about Frank, Sammy, Elvis, and others, which really caused a stir.

After my family and I had settled in Palm Springs and Danny had become a "close" friend of Frank's, they decided to buy a Gulfstream II. It was a three-way split, as the purchase included Mickey Rudrin, Frank's lawyer. Danny sold the Lear, and I was let go. Art (the wife abuser)remained as cocaptain on the G-II, along with Frank's chief pilot, Johnny Spoths. This didn't last very long, however. Danny found Art at the bar in Jilly's Saloon in New York one night. Danny suggested that he leave before Frank saw him there. Art took offense to this. The encounter escalated to a fistfight between the two. Art was fired on the spot. After working with a couple of temporary pilots to replace

Art, Johnny offered me the copilot position on the G-2. After some soul-searching and deliberation about whether we should continue to starve or if I should accept a good-paying job with Sinatra Enterprises, I decided to accept, while trying not to appear too grateful and relieved.

Frank's friend and bodyguard, Jilly Rizzo, had a restaurant and bar, Jilly's, in New York. He also built a Jilly's in Palm Springs. Dottye and I had dinner at Jilly's several times. Once we were there, in a booth across from Sinatra's private booth. We were talking about Sinatra when I noticed he had just sat down with some friends. I asked Dottye, "How would you like to see him in person?" Dottye's fork was on the way to her mouth when she saw him. It was a perfect moment: She froze with the fork midway to her mouth and could not move. Sinatra saw this and asked his friends who the girl was with the "frozen fork." They explained that she was one of the pilots' wives. Dottye had two other encounters with Sinatra. Once, during one of his Buick commercials at Jilly's, she stepped on his foot by mistake in the crowd. The other came when we were flying then-Governor Ronald Reagan from Santa Monica to Palm Springs in the Gulfstream. We were running late, and Dottye got a little uneasy and called the hanger, expecting to reach the mechanic for information about the flight. Frank answered the phone. When the unmistakable voice said, "Hello?" Dottye froze. He said, "Who is this?" With no idea what to say, she said, "Has the hangar landed yet? This is Lee's wife, Dottye." Sinatra said, "Aw, honey, are you worried? They have just landed and are taxiing in now." When the plane's door opened, he ran up the stairs and said, "Lee, call your wife, she's worried!" We had a number of celebrities on board during the Learjet and Gulfstream years. One humorous event took place after a flight with Burt Lancaster. Burt had stumbled off the plane, not sober, jumped into his convertible sports car, and raced onto the taxiway at the Palm Springs airport. Joe, the flight engineer, climbed onto the aircraft tug and chased after him, as it was pitch-black and there was still air traffic around the field. It took a while, as the tug was no match for Burt's car, but Joe finally corralled him back to the hangar. Thankfully, Frank had left before this took place.

Flights on Sinatra's plane were always interesting. He would frequently come up to the cockpit and chat with us, tell a joke, or just talk. On a trip from London to Nice, our passenger was Princess Grace. I was invited into the cabin to meet her. She was very nice and gracious, though I can't remember what she said. California governor Ronald Reagan took some trips with us. Henry Kissinger, Lucile Ball, and others also took trips with us. On one flight to New York from London, about midway over the Atlantic, we felt the plane rocking and lurching a little. An investigation of the cabin revealed dense cigarette smoke and loud music, some of it from Trini Lopez and his guitar. The rest of the passengers I don't remember, but it was like a who's who from the jazz world. We made a few trips to Acapulco. Once while there, we got a call that Mr. S had to leave immediately. Things don't happen too fast in Mexico, so the flight plan didn't get processed in time. We bribed the guard at the back gate of the airport to open for the limousine. The limo came to a stop at the plane's stairs, and Frank, Jilly, and others scrambled aboard, saying, "Let's get the hell out of here now!" Sensing the urgency and knowing the control tower had no flight plan on us, we announced that we were taxiing to the runway. We did so, despite the protests from the tower. If you have a choice between defying the Mexican authorities and making Frank Sinatra very angry, you keep going and get the hell out of Acapulco. No truck appeared to block the runway, and no Mexican Air National Guard planes were deployed to challenge us, so we took off and had an uneventful flight to Los Angeles International Airport. We did have to file a flight plan upon entry into U.S. airspace. Another time, we had to fly to Acapulco to rescue Mr. Sinatra, but that was before the escape with no flight plan. The reason for the rapid departures was usually that he'd had some encounter with the press that turned out badly.

Looking back, it seems exciting, but it still didn't compare with flying low over North Vietnam, trying to outrun a flock of SAMs missiles. That will get your pulse up.

The Sinatra years with the Gulfstream II, "Sunbird," ended after he stopped performing. The aircraft was sold and the crew went job-hunting again. I flew a Learjet out of Palm Springs. It was a charter operation that occasionally would fly Mr. Sinatra, since I knew the secretary who booked his flights. It was during that time that Dottye and I owned a home in Palm Springs. We lived in the Deepwell neighborhood, which also had William Holden, the Gabor sisters, Jerry Lewis, and other celebrities. The kids came home one day with some long bird feathers and a few oranges. They had chased this tall bird around until they apparently found its home. The owner came out and thanked the kids for bringing his African crowned crane home. A friend later explained that the owner was William Holden, the actor who made frequent trips to Africa. He gave them the feathers and oranges as a thank-you gift.

One Halloween, we drove the kids around Tamarisk Golf Course, where Frank and Danny lived. Although they didn't get much from most of the houses, one door opened and there was Red Skelton behind it. He took them in and loaded them up with great treats. He picked Chip up and held him, explaining that his son had died, but would have been Chip's age. Red would drive his Rolls around Palm Springs with a wreath attached to the front grill. He liked to stop and chat with just anybody. Celebrities did not get mobbed or followed by the paparazzi in Palm Springs. There was a general understanding that it was their home, so no one bothered them.

After Danny Schwartz sold his Learjet but before I was offered the Sinatra job, there was a period of time when I started painting professionally. I taught painting at our house and sold paintings through some galleries in Los Angeles and Santa Barbara. I even had a worthless agent who took the pieces to the galleries. They asked for owls and eagles, which I soon hated to paint, but did a lot of anyway. Carlo Walhbeck, a local but successful surrealist painter whose paintings were in LA and New York, helped and encouraged me. Carlo lived in the previous home of Douglas Fairbanks Jr, a fabulous house on the side of the San Jacinto Mountains. It had a tramcar that went from the house down to the pool. We enjoyed visiting and swimming with them. Carlo and his wife Barbara would also visit us where we lived in the Deepwell area of Palm Springs. I soon realized that I was not making enough with my artwork, so I bought a small building specialties shop called Desert Building Specialties. I had to learn to lay floor tile and install barbeque and fireplace equipment. I also laid gas pipe underground. It was during that time, while laying floor tile in a ballroom for the Hearst family – of publishing fame - that Mrs. Hearst invited me to their New Year's Eve party. Dottye and I were also having a New Year's Eve party, but decided to leave our party to attend this once-in-a-lifetime event at the Hearst mansion. I don't need to say we were somewhat out of our element there, but the Hearsts took us under their wings, chatting with us away from the group. The press was there, of course. But our big thrill came when Hoagy Carmichael came through the front door with his arms full of champagne. Hoagy, the composer of "Stardust," became the life of the party. Sadly, we had to leave to rejoin our own party. The well-dressed parking valets were happy to give us back our modest ride.

I installed gas fire logs at Liberace's home, "the Cloisters," as well as fire screens at Sinatra's and his mother Dolly's homes. Dolly seemed to be a good person, but did not take anything from Frank or his buddies. I witnessed a rather profound argument while there. Zeppo Marx, one of the Marx brothers who was not well known, became a friend of mine, although we never got together for anything. He promised to take me out on his boat, which we never got to do. He had recently been divorced from his wife, a former showgirl who later married Frank. She wasn't a very kind person. She isolated Frank from his children, so that they did not see him very often. Even when Frank became ill and was hospitalized in later years, she kept his family away.

We only flew Elvis twice, but we often carried Colonel Parker, his agent-manager. Usually, Parker would take our Gulfstream and Elvis took an F-28 private jet. The F-28 had more room for him and his somewhat unruly gang of musicians, who were known to carry a variety of weapons that they would play with during the trip. I was content with Col. Parker's entourage; after all, I had already seen enough combat.

When the Gulfstream was sold, I started work as chief pilot of the Desert Jet Air Taxi Service at the Palm Springs airport. A few years earlier, I'd had an old WWII trainer airplane at that airport. It was a Ryan PT-22, which had open cockpits, a Kinner 55 radial engine, no battery, no radio, and a wooden propeller that someone had to spin to start the engine. This meant no communication with the Palm Springs tower. I made all my movements, including takeoff and landing, only after receiving a green or red light signal from the tower. I would put my daughter, Carol, and son Chip together in the front cockpit and I would fly from the rear cockpit. I referred to the PT-22 as the "Orange Crate" due to its age and condition, but the kids called it "the Orange Grape," as that was what my nickname for it sounded like. The only required equipment to fly it was a rag to wipe the engine oil off the windshield.

One evening the phone rang at our home in Palm Springs; it was Dionne, a woman who worked with the charter company at the airport. She was excited. She said she had met a man who said he was Samuel Goldwyn's grandson, Sean Goldwyn. He claimed that he was making a movie about his life and wanted Dionne's son to play the part of him in the movie. He also said he needed a pilot to manage the aircraft he was buying. That's when she thought of me. The man agreed to meet with me to decide if the arrangement would work. I thought it wouldn't hurt to speak with him. The meeting was arranged, a limousine showed up at our house, and Dottye and I were taken to his house in Palm Springs. Dionne, her son, and the man's attorney were waiting there. We talked for some time about his plans for the movie and the airplane he expected to have. All of it made sense, but a couple of things bothered us. First, the guy was missing a tooth, which was odd since he should have the money to have that corrected, second, Dottye noticed he said, "Money is a tool to be used." She had read a book, *The Moguls*, in which that same phrase was used. Anyway, in the next few days I was given a written contract for my proposed services as a pilot. I showed this proposal to Danny Schwartz; he said it looked good to him and I should consider taking it. More time passed, and when I spoke again with Dionne, she seemed very nervous, almost frightened, about the situation with her son. We had a friend who was a police detective. I explained the whole story and only asked if he could check on Samuel

Goldwyn's grandson for me. Joe, the detective, called me in a day or so to say that Goldwyn did have a grandson, but he was living in Boston and looked nothing like this guy. I was really beginning to be concerned for Dionne and her boy. Joe could not get a warrant to search the man's house. Joe was about six foot one and 250 pounds, and pretty much fearless. So, on his own, he went to the door and rang the bell. When the chauffeur opened the door, Joe could see in a mirror in the hall that "Sean Goldwyn" was hiding behind the front door. Joe grabbed the man's hand as if to shake it, saying, "Hello, my name is Joe Jones…" Once inside, he took them both into custody. They did not resist. What he found inside, besides a very frightened Dionne and her son, was a briefcase containing a hash pipe and several notes demanding money from banks. Dionne said the chauffeur had gone to buy champagne to celebrate the "arrangement." Joe said the plan was to spike the champagne for Dionne with PCP, then leave town with a number of things, such as money for the bogus stock certificates they had sold. It seems these two were ex-cons who had been doing this gig in several states. They would invent a story and situation to gain the trust of the victims and then would coerce money or valuables from them. At the same time, they would sell fake stock certificates around the town. They had been in prison for similar crimes. When our phone rings, it is often the beginning of a new adventure.

One year, Dottye took Carol and Chip to a celebrity golf game that Bob Hope, Clint Eastwood, Peter Faulk, and Buddy Hackett were playing in. The kids had never witnessed a golf game. During the game, Hackett and others were at a green, putting, when Hackett overshot the green. The ball rolled down the slope and came to rest near Carol. So Carol, thinking she was being helpful, picked up the ball and tried to return it to Hackett. Hackett saw this as an opportunity to be comical and started chasing Carol around the green while swinging his putter over his head in a mock rage. After a few minutes, it ended, and he gave Carol and Chip each a ball. The crowd had a big laugh at the episode.

Desert Jet Air Taxi Service consisted of a Learjet, an MU-2 and a Twin Cessna. It was a pleasant and peaceful flight operation, with domestic trips, an occasional flight to Mexico, and a few trips to LA or Burbank with Sinatra (usually just him). I got the Sinatra trips because I knew Dorothy, his secretary, who made the transportation arrangements. Then one day the whole thing changed. Margaret Mead—a pilot, not the author—walked into my office to ask if I would be interested in going to Italy. She hardly got the words out when I said yes! Of course, I was not thinking about my house, my car, my schoolteacher wife, my small specialty store, or the sailboat moored in a slip at Dana Point two and a half hours from Palm Springs. Adventure with a capital A overshadowed everything, including common sense.

Not one pilot in my office was willing to go to Italy as my copilot, so Margaret suggested I talk to a young pilot from Long Beach whom she knew. Margaret explained that an Italian family would be leasing the Learjet for one year while they waited for a new Learjet, which was being built at the factory in Wichita, Kansas. So I called the pilot Margaret suggested. He had no jet experience and almost no foreign travel experience, but he was very interested in going with me. So, after briefly discussing the terms, I literally hired Mike Reaney over the phone, sight unseen. Luckily, Mike was a fast learner and was comfortable in the aircraft about halfway to Italy.

Dottye was teaching an elementary school class when I left Palm Springs, so I couldn't tell her directly that we had to leave quickly. I left a message that we were leaving and she and the kids could join me in Italy—of course, when she could do something with the house, the car, the business, the sailboat, and a major surgery that one of our Carol needed to correct a thorasic condition It was amazing and I still don't know how, but she did it all and joined me in Turin , Italy, in less than four months.

CHAPTER 7

Italy

After fuel stops in Nova Scotia, Greenland, Iceland and Belgium, we arrived in Turin and met the Bugnone family. Aldo was the father and CEO of an aluminum production company. Piero, his oldest son, ran the company, assisted by Alberto, Piero's younger brother. Aldo's daughter, Valeria, had nothing to do with the company, which involved the production of aluminum. They built aluminum factories that would take raw materials such as bauxite, melt it, roll it into sheets, stretch it, and turn out things like trays, plates, containers, and even film. There were even looms that would produce clothing containing threads of shiny aluminum—quite stylish for 1973. Most of their customers were Eastern Bloc countries, including Bulgaria, Poland, Czechoslovakia, Yugoslavia, Romania, Greece, the UK, and Russia. Aldo's wife, Teresa, was the real boss of the family, a quiet woman with an iron will.

I never knew how many villas the family owned, but I did get to see two, one near the factory in Turin and another at Portofino. Both were big, old, and completely staffed with maids, cooks, butlers, and chauffeurs. I can never forget Giovani, a chauffeur for the family who had served during WWII. He had been captured and spent years in a prison in Kenya. He spoke Swahili as well as Italian, but no English. He was a kind, quiet man of about seventy, with an unshakable loyalty to the family. Aldo was always dressed in a suit and tie, fastidiously clean and neat, but always good-natured and humorous. I remember him stretched on the Portofino dock beside several other people, who were all in swimsuits. Of course, he was in his well-pressed suit and tie. It was as if he was standing at attention while lying there, feet together, smiling and joking with the others, quite at ease and not in the least embarrassed. Aldo started with nothing, selling burlap bags. In time, he developed a business and became an inventor. One of his inventions was the textile loom that produced clothing with aluminum threads woven into it. He also became politically powerful and acquired the title of "Cavaliere di Lavoro," or "Knight of Labor." He had great influence on the government in Rome. Whenever I had a problem with my Italian license or the plane, his favorite expression was, "We will move someone in Rome." The problem always disappeared. Sometimes, locally, it was easier to lubricate the path with money. The Bugnones offered me a permanent position as chief pilot for the new Learjet, which I accepted. My family and I stayed for four years in Italy.

Mike went home but got qualified with a type rating in Learjet in Wichita Kansas Learjet factory. Pier Carlo Busato, a very young man experienced in aerial photography in Nepal and Tunisia, was hired as the new copilot.. He was also a racecar driver and a member of the Italian ski team.

We took a trip to Sofia, Bulgaria. While at an Orbis hotel for lunch, we met a small orchestra group. They were young people—probably university students. They spoke no English, but I got across to them that I wanted them to play "Fascination." They didn't understand, so I hummed a few bars for them while they were on break. When they started to play again—usually classical—they played a beautiful rendition of "Fascination." I was amazed, and we showed them we appreciated it! We went several times to Krakow, Poland, an interesting city with nice, friendly people. While walking downtown early one evening, we could hear classical music coming from inside a restaurant. We went into the crowded restaurant and found a small string ensemble playing for a very appreciative crowd. It was very different from our American culture. I'll never forget our weather briefing in Krakow before a flight to Italy. The weather agent must have taken forty-five minutes to explain what the weather should be like throughout the whole route. This was complete with pictures he drew himself, in color, of all clouds expected. It was so different from, for example, Geneva, where they may hand you a computer weather report of maybe three to four lines.

On a trip to Bucharest, Romania, with Mike in the leased Learjet, we arrived just before a state ceremony at which the head of state from an African country was about to arrive. They would not let us stay on the main ramp with our US-registered Learjet, so they had a guard board the aircraft and escort us to a remote taxiway, where we stayed until the event was over. We did get to see a low-level flyby of three or four MiG-17s, but not much else

In some places, like Luxor, Egypt, we had to climb the stairs, outside, to file a flight plan in the control tower. On one flight to Luxor, we arrived very early—about three thirty am local time. No customs, no immigration, no handling service, only the tower operator and someone cleaning the terminal were around. We waited until about six am, when Egypt Air's scheduled flight came in, then the airport terminal became a beehive of activity. The hotel had lost our reservations and said they were "full," but we argued and bribed for another two to three hours before getting very comfortable accommodations. I was learning the secrets of international operations, patience, tolerance and bribes. Patience and tolerance make you feel better; bribes make things happen.

The Bugnones were happy to have Dottye go with us on trips (Greece, Egypt, Iran, et cetera) because when she came, it seemed like they got the contracts they wanted. After returning from one of our Tehran trips, Piero Bugnone said, "We made so much (US $60 million) that we could just leave the engines running." Our life in Italy was good, very much the adventure each day. We enrolled David, our youngest, in the local elementary school, where no one spoke English. I was learning Italian and tried to negotiate with the principal, a lady who was pleasant, but insisted that his US records be officially translated. After more than one visit and attempt, we had them translated at the US consulate in Turin, where they decorated the documents with stamps, wax, and ribbons. That did it. The principal was bubbling over. Still, we later took him out and put him in the local American school, where his mother had the duty of teaching him. Chip went to an American school in Milan, staying with a family there. Carol was enrolled in a Catholic school in Rome, which she hated but which seemed the only solution for her at her age as no local schools were available. I would fly to Rome a lot, and had a driver, Gino, who would get me at the airport and take me to Carol's school to visit.

Dinners at the Villa, a Bugnone compound near Turin, were very special. There were many servants wearing white gloves; the whole affair was really formal.

Dottye got food poisoning while on a trip in Tehran. She was very sick during the flight back to Turin, during which Aldo held her hand and comforted her.

All of Italy shuts down for the month of August. It is called "Ferragosto". One August, I drove the family down to Bari on the east coast, where we took the ferry over to Greece and drove around Athens and Delphi. Dottye was very uncomfortable at Delphi; she felt as though she had been there before and had a bad experience. The loading and unloading of the ferry was like a destruction derby on steroids. Noise, dust, confusion, and no courtesy!

On the last part of our Ferragosto trip, we took the ferry to the Greek island of Corfu, where I had arranged for a rental apartment in a village called Pelekas. It was a three- or four-story building still under construction, and our apartment was on the second floor. We learned after our arrival that the bathroom was shared by the Black Bat Restaurant on the ground floor. Otherwise, the accommodations were, in my opinion, rustic and quaint." However, Dottye's description was a profound "primitive!" This difference in perception did little to enhance the vacation atmosphere. Nor did my beach experience with the kids. Pelekas was at the top of an olive-tree-covered hill. The Ionian Sea could be reached by a hike down the hill and through pretty dense vegetation. Chip, David, and I were joined by their newfound friend, a German girl of about ten years old. When we finally broke through the tall weeds, a beautiful beach was displayed before us. There were many young people playing on the beach and in the water—perfect, except none of them was wearing a stich of clothing. The image somehow remains in my mind of a girl, who at our first encounter of this scene, was doing cartwheels in the sand. The shock of this immediately put me into denial ("This can't be happening!"), from which I quickly recovered and ushered the kids behind a big rock. The kids took it pretty well, in all with minimal psychological damage.

We did have a great experience in Corfu, in spite of the beach issue. The women of Pelekas were dressed all in black, much like nuns. Each of them had to examine Dottye closely. We realized that they were amazed that she had teeth, for it seemed there was not one full set of teeth among the women of Pelekas!

The ferry trip and drive back to Turin were less eventful, except for our stop at a small hilltop town near Siena, Italy, where they were engaged in a Palio, a race that occurs twice during the summer each year. During the races, everyone dresses and acts like medieval folks and cheers for their teams. The teams race against each other, riding or chasing horses, donkeys, goats or other animals through the village. We never learned about the prize, if there was one. But the crowd was in a frenzy, especially when the animals or their chaser would wipe out on a turn, sending chasers, animals, and spectators sailing or scrambling for safety. I think perhaps there was also a bit of drinking going on.

Back home in our apartment in Revigliasco, near Turin, we settled into our routine: me waiting to fly, Dottye teaching, David attending school, Chip in the American school in Milan, and Carol in Rome.

The trains were wonderful in Italy, as well as all of Europe. We went to Rome on one occasion, staying at a very small hotel near St. Peter's Basilica. On the train on the way back, I realized we left our passports at the hotel, where they kept them in the safe as a customary procedure. I got off the train, caught a train back to Rome, retrieved the passports, then returned to Turin.

Pier Carlo's parents lived on a farm about forty miles north of Turin, close to the old Roman settlement of Magnano. We became friends with them and would stay overnight at their home. I would sit for hours with his father, drinking Grappa or sweet vermouth and trying to talk to him in Italian. He had lost a leg while fighting in Greece during WWII, but got around very well. He built the house and compound at the farm, mostly by himself. Pier Carlo's mother was Parisian French and a great cook. However, we never got comfortable eating the excellent roast rabbit because it was taken from their collection of rabbits in the barn. Pier Carlo made it worse by calling the dish "bunny," which tickled him greatly. He would say, "We're having bunny for dinner."

Our first home in Italy was in a village near Turin called Pino Torinese. It was steeped in Roman history, with wonderful small shops, bakeries—which made the world-famous Torino grissini, or breadsticks—antiques, and restaurants. One very well-known restaurant was the Pigna d'Oro, a pretty expensive place that was frequented by celebrities. One night, while we were there, I was at their very small bar, which had enough space to seat perhaps four comfortably. The guy next to me looked familiar, but I couldn't place him. I finally decided he was the plumber who had done some work at the apartment. Later, the proprietor, Pietro, asked if I had enjoyed meeting Marcello Mastroianni. No wonder he looked familiar, since I'd seen him in a lot of movies. He had been very friendly, just chatting and making small talk. He must have been amused that I obviously didn't recognize him.

The aircraft that I first had in Italy, the leased Learjet 24, had a very peculiar problem. If a passenger sneezed, even in the back seat, the aircraft would make a sudden pitching oscillation, or "porpoising" maneuver. The defect had been occurring for months, as no one could correct it or even find out what caused it. It had to be associated with the autopilot, since it only happened in auto flight. There were other defects that the Swiss maintenance service could not address, so I decided to take the aircraft to Nuremberg, Germany, where a Learjet service with a good reputation was located. The Learjet manager, Helmut Shoeneville, said for me to wait in the lounge while he looked into the autopilot problem. About twenty-five minutes later he came into the lounge, holding up a small metal tube and saying, "This is your problem." It had a very small crack in it, which was positioned near the outflow valve that allows air from the cabin to escape. The tube connected open ports to the altitude controller, so when any extra air pressure, such as a cough or sneeze, occurred, the extra pressure was felt through the outflow valve and onto this cracked line. The altitude controller sensed this as a change in pressure, so the autopilot was simply trying to correct for the change. I was sufficiently impressed and continued to bring my Learjets to Helmut for all maintenance and repairs. Even years later, when flying out of Istanbul, we went to Nuremberg. Dottye went with me on some of those trips. Christmastime in Nuremberg was very special, and a very big deal indeed. There were open-air markets, decorations, and of course the world-famous glockenspiel, an animated clock almost like an elaborate cuckoo clock. The old town part of Nuremberg goes back to medieval times and is preserved as such with cobblestone streets, towers, walls, and parapets. It is an absolutely charming place and was a favorite of ours.

We took a family trip to Nice, France, and had dinner on Grande Corniche at a place called La Ferme de St. Michel (St. Michael's Farm). It was a once-in-a-lifetime experience. They over-feed you with farm-fresh food of all kinds, plus the atmosphere was one of such exuberance and joy that it was contagious. Each of us felt the individual attention. The waiters teased and cajoled, keeping you entertained most of the time. Overindulgence doesn't quite describe the experience. It is a place none of us will forget.

The four years we spent in Italy were full of adventures and unforgettable people and places. I was able to do a lot of drawing and some painting while not out on trips—and sometimes when on a trip, but waiting for our passengers. Italy had an inexhaustible amount of subject matter: fountains, buildings, churches, landscapes, and more.

We moved from Pino Torinese to Revigliasco; this was a true Roman settlement, like no place I've ever seen. We lived in a modern, new apartment duplex, overlooking the town. The building's architect lived two doors down from us. Our favorite restaurant in Revigliasco, L'Osto (The Host), was run by a family, from the chef to the waiter. This was the best food you could find in Italy, not fancy or exotic, but really good! The area was full of cherry trees, some just outside our windows. The view was to the southwest, with a breathtaking panorama of the Italian Alps, just on the eastern border of France.

When I had some time off in the winter, we would go up to the Gressoney-Saint-Jean, northwest of Turin and near the Swiss border. We had a rental apartment there, and we would all ski: Dottye and I, cross-country, Chip and David downhill. The two of us enrolled in the cross-country school, which held competitions on the local track. I did win one of the races, despite falling twice, but second place was likely a handicapped person anyway. Chip went on to win downhill competitions in Austria and Switzerland; he was a natural. Can you imagine saying, "I learned to ski in the Swiss Alps"?

One of my first memories after we started regular flights in and out of Turin-Caselle Airport was arriving at after midnight and before we shut down, the tower operator asked us to report to the tower before leaving the airport. As we entered, they were having a wild party, but the smell was awful. They were cooking a specialty of the region called bagna càuda, the main ingredients of which were wine and garlic— heavy on the garlic. After raising hell for some time with the tower guys, I made my way home. I swear as I opened the door, Dottye said, "What is that smell?" It took several days to expunge the odor of the bagna càuda from my skin!

The company made several trips to Tehran, Iran. They were trying to make a contract with the Black Princess, the Shah's sister. In fact, they did manage a $60 million contract there and would bring suitcases full of money back to Italy. When returning from Iran, we could not take the most direct route through Turkey and Greece because the Greeks and Turks would not allow traffic across their mutual borders during those years. We had to go by way of Beirut, Lebanon, where we could refuel. Sometimes, you could hear explosions from the conflicts they were having near the airport. Most of the airport officials were not very friendly. The Learjet 25 we flew was US-registered aircraft and was recognized as such at all airports we used.. US aircraft were not generally welcome in the "iron curtain' countries, but "officially" we were welcome because the company was usually dealing with a top government agent, such as the minister of heavy industry.

One trip to Moscow was scheduled the day after we returned from Iran, so I had no chance to obtain a Russian visa. The Bugnone family asked if I was willing to go anyway. Of course, with my unquenchable thirst for adventure, I agreed to go. Somehow my Italian copilot, Pier

Carlo, had a visa already. We flew first to Warsaw, Poland, where we picked up our "Russian" navigator, Stanislas. He was a radio operator for Aeroflot, a Russian airline. Stanislas spoke zero English or Italian, so he was pretty much a "decoration" on board our flight. His official job was to make sure we did not fly over sensitive Russian areas or photograph anything. Actually, the commendatore was such a gracious host that he saw to it that Stanislas consumed a substantial amount of vodka, rendering him unable to navigate himself to the cockpit, much less monitor our actions. We could have buzzed the Kremlin and he would have had no idea. Arriving at Sheremetyevo Airport in Moscow, I grabbed Stanislas to help me get by the security police. Aldo persuaded the officials, so they just took my passport and sent me on my way. I didn't see it again until we left Moscow a few days later.

In Moscow, we stayed at the Europa Hotel, which had a thousand rooms. I was able to take taxis, buses, trolleys, and the subway without restrictions or being followed (I think). On a whim, I boarded a subway at Red Square. Thinking I was smart, I wrote down the name over one of the gates, which I assumed was the name of the station. I rode for fifteen minutes in one direction, boarded a train going the opposite way, timed the same fifteen minutes, saw the same sign, got off, and emerged victoriously at Red Square. That night I was relating my adventure to the commendatore and others when Ponzano, the one of our group who spoke Russian, asked to see the name of the station that I had noted. Ponzano said, "That word is exit." But for my timing the train ride, I could have found myself in St. Petersburg, or somewhere else, very lost.

The subway in Moscow is like nowhere else. It has very large crystal chandeliers, and tile walls and ceilings. It is really clean.

While in Moscow, Pier Carlo and I went out to the airport to look around. Because we were in uniform, we were not stopped or questioned. We went right out on the flight line, which had military as well as civilian aircraft. We even went to the control tower, where we climbed the stairs to the top and were amazed by what we saw. Seated at a very big desk was the tower commander. He was in an impressive black uniform with huge epaulettes and many rows of medals on his chest. He had massive silver hair and a grandiose manner that would have done justice to any movie or novel featuring such a character. Fortunately, he was very friendly, and with very limited English, tried to show us around. I was a little concerned about being in Russia so soon after leaving the Air Force—after all, I had been in the Air Force Strategic Air command. My target had been the Kremlin. My limited knowledge of the "war plans" might have been of interest to Russia. The Cold War was still showing signs of life in 1974 when we were in Russia. In later trips to Russia and ex-Soviet countries like Kazakhstan, we stayed at places that were previously KGB facilities. Never was I ever contacted by security police or KGB, so I must have been of little interest to them. It is true, however, that in most Russian hotels, if you are in your room and loudly say something about getting your laundry done, someone will show up at your door very soon afterwards to collect it.

Four years went rapidly in Italy. We make many flights to Geneva with Piero Bugnone, the son of the CEO, Aldo and the primary boss of company operations. One day, we were scheduled to take Piero to Geneva, Switzerland, but after waiting for him for several hours at Turin airport, he had not shown up. When I called the office, Piero said to fly the plane to Geneva and call him when we got there. That seemed strange, as he had never asked for that before. When I called him from

Geneva, he said to leave the plane there and drive back to Turin by rental car. We did this, and I hurried to his office when we got back. He explained everything. The Italian customs service was aware that the plane, although registered as a US aircraft, was in fact owned by Bugnone. Piero had tried to hide this by having the ownership papers signed by Hunter Engineering of Riverside, California. Hunter was part of the Italian company's holdings. Bugnone avoided paying tax on the plane this way. Piero said the customs officials had warned him to get the plane out of the country or they would have to confiscate it. They had already seized one of the Agusta Bell's planes in Rome, and another had escaped before being seized as well. Augusta had registered their planes in Lichtenstein, which had no tax. That's as much of the story as I know. I'm sure there was more to it.

I asked Piero what I should do about the Learjet. He said we had to sell it, He would not pay the tax on it. but I should stay. They might get another plane later.

So I went about trying to sell the plane, first while it was in Geneva. Later, I flew it back to the US to try to sell it there. Since the plane had always been registered in the US, it could not have been exported— therefore, no import should have been necessary. But as I was getting settled in a Denver airport hotel, I got a call from two government agents, who asked why I had brought an aircraft into the US without proper importation. I explained the situation well enough to avoid being taken into custody, but was told to go directly to US customs at the airport. When I walked into the customs, an agent was waiting for me with a list of Charles Smiths, which is the name on my passport. Lee is my nickname. all of whom were wanted for felonies such as narcotics smuggling, kidnapping, and murder. I think he asked, "Which one of these is you?" I tried to appear upstanding, but he said the main issue was failure to import the plane. I tried to explain that it was never exported, therefore it shouldn't need to be imported since it was still US-registered. If you have ever dealt with government officials—especially US customs—you know that you being right is not something that is generally allowed? I was directed to a customs "broker" to import the machine. I did so, but during the application, we came to the part about the value of the import. When I mentioned $1.1 million, the broker when into shock, saying it would take at least five brokers to commit to such a cost as one could only meet a $200,000 committment So I dejectedly returned to the customs office, where the agent was slowly turning the pages of some manual. Seeing me, he said, "Oh, there you are. You know, Captain, there is no requirement for you to import that plane." So I was out of there is less than a minute, with no paperwork, release, or anything else, as far as I remember.

I did sell the airplane and return to Italy, where I remained for about five months with full pay and living expenses. Finally, one day, I went to see Piero. I told him that although I was grateful for his family's kindness and generosity, I had to return to actually being a pilot. He understood and we said our goodbyes.

CHAPTER 8

Learjet Factory, 1977–1978

Later we returned to the US, where I got a job as an instructor and demonstration pilot for the Learjet factory in Tucson, Arizona. I got the job because they needed a multilingual pilot, especially one with Spanish capabilities. My Spanish amounted to some courses in college and a Spanish tape that I listened to, so it was a stretch. But I wanted the job, and what the heck, I knew Italian.

When I started the job in Tucson, the first pilots they gave me to train were from the Argentine Air Force. They spoke no English at all, and their Spanish was Castilian, which might as well have been Swahili as I could understand none of it. The first few flights with them were a little different. I asked them if they could understand me. They said yes, they could. So I told them to do exactly what I said during flight, don't bother to speak, and we will sort it out later. We got through the training OK, but after they were ready to fly their new Learjet back to Argentina, I still was not happy with their instrument flying, so it was decided that I would fly with them back to their base at Paraná, Entre Ríos, Argentina. We flew through Lima, Peru, where we stayed overnight. The next morning, I discovered they had left Lima without me, taking the plane to Argentina. I was shocked, angry, and frustrated, and I called the general at Paraná. He apologized profusely and said I would understand when I got to Paraná. He could not explain on the phone. After I arrived on a commercial flight, learned that the plane, which was a special photographic model, flew over Chile on the way to Argentina, taking pictures. It was a tactical flight, and they could not have me, a US citizen, exposed to possible ground fire. I was received graciously at Paraná, where I completed the training. After a day or so in Buenos Aires, I left for the US. Again by commercial airlines. The next Spanish-speakers were from Mexico and other Latin American countries, so the language thing was less stressful as it was a more familiar form of Spanish.

While returning to Tucson from Argentina, I had a layover in Rio de Janiero. I decided to take a dip in the Atlantic. Reaching the beautiful beach near the hotel, I took off my jeans, rolled up my wallet and sunglasses in the jeans and shirt, and walked a few yards into the water. I was about knee-deep when I thought about my things, so I turned around and saw a boy of about fifteen holding up my jeans with my wallet and sunglasses tumbling out into the sand. In a rage, I began running toward him. He dropped the jeans, grabbed what I thought was my wallet, and began sprinting for the street that ran by the beach. The chase went about like you would think with a forty-three-year-old after a fifteen-year-old. Even so, with my adrenaline soaring, I wasn't doing too badly. After winding through heavy traffic with the thief about fifty yards ahead, I spotted a policeman. Getting his attention, but not knowing Portuguese, I screamed, "Ladro, ladro," and pointed at the boy. The cop understood and the two of us continued the chase. Then the cop stopped a passing cab and we both climbed in to continue the chase. After a block or two, we lost sight of the boy and abandoned the chase. I made my way, clad in my swim trunks only, to the beach, where I expected to find my clothes with no wallet. Instead, I found the jeans and shirt just where the boy had dropped them, and my wallet with everything inside, exposed and surrounded by a rather large group of sunbathers who seem to have ignored it all. It was pure dumb luck that only my sunglasses were missing.

One of the challenges of being a demo pilot was demonstrating the new Learjet in other countries. I flew one trip through South America, crossing the South Atlantic from Recife, Brazil and landing in Sierra Leone for refueling. This was my first exposure to places of extreme poverty. I quickly realized how privileged I had been all my life. From Sierra Leone, we went to Ghana to show the aircraft to someone, I don't recall who. Then we flew to Lagos, Nigeria. The very name causes me to recoil and painful memories to come back. We were supposed to meet the salesman for the demo in Lagos, but he was not there to meet us and we had no number or address. So we checked with the airport hotel; it was fully booked, as was every other Lagos hotel that night. Finally, a hotel clerk suggested the Mount Pleasant Guest House. Desperate, we made our way there by taxi. It was dark, which is the only reason we did not turn around and go back to stay in the Learjet for the night. I doubt if I can describe the course of the night. Unidentifiable noises and unpleasant odors dominated the evening hours. Morning came none too soon to reveal a horrific scene. "Filthy" is the closest in English to describe the room. I won't even try to describe the bathroom.

Needless to say, a shower or bath was not in the plan, but an expeditious checkout worked for us. My copilot, a former New Orleans Saints football player, was ready to jump ship if accommodations didn't improve drastically. We did locate the salesman, who had reservations for us the day we arrived at the EKU Holiday Inn—which, compared with the Mt. Pleasant Guest House, was the Palace of Versailles. One local flight while in Lagos was to some small airport in northern Nigeria. It was nothing fancy there, but you did have to check the runways often, as people or camels would occupy parts of them, just wandering. I found the animals easier to predict than the humans—I think because the animals consumed less alcohol and were more mentally stable. During the Mt. Pleasant Guest House night, someone with a tug ran into a tip tank on the Learjet, a hit and run, I guess, as no one would accept responsibility for it. My attempts to protest abated after I noticed the automatic weapon resting on the table near us. So, we left for Egypt, our next stop. The distance was too great for our fuel load, so we stopped in Chad, about midway to Egypt. While in Chad, we caught a glimpse of the French Foreign Legion marching in formation while we were waiting for fuel. Fuel and landing fees were always cash in these countries, and as always, an automatic weapon rested on the table between the agent and me.. Luxor, Egypt, had better conditions, cleaner and more civilized. We still had to climb an outdoor ladder to reach the tower when filing a fight plan, but the tower folks were nice enough and helpful. After the demo there, we went to Saudi Arabia, and then to Doha, United Arab Emirates, where we flew the Sheik of Qatar to Kuwait for an overnight. The copilot and I were invited to the client's compound. Once inside we were shocked to see a fully stocked bar with booze freely flowing, in a country that prohibited any and all alcoholic drinks. Our next stop was Bahrain for about two days. Bahrain had an open drinking and dancing policy, and the hotel bar was a popular hangout for the Saudis, who could go there and tie one on with no one complaining. My copilot, the football player, had a drinking problem that wasn't working out very well. He could get hostile after drinking a while—never to me, but he picked on an East German who happened to be there making an ass of himself. My copilot claimed that he could kill him so quick, he'd be dead when he hit the floor. I could see this was not going to end well and wanted to see the end of our trip without losing our freedom. So I convinced him to leave the bar. He did not stop the drinking, however, and I had concerns about his functionality the next day. This turned out to be the end of our part of the demo tour, as another crew came over to continue the trip.

While in Tucson with the Learjet factory, I was offered a job as chief pilot of an operation in Saudi Arabia. I would be flying a Learjet 35 in support of the F-15 program there. I would be employed by the Harris Corporation in Melbourne, Florida. I was to hire two more pilots and a mechanic, which I did—but we never got to Saudi Arabia. After I hired the crew, they left their jobs, I left Learjet, and I arrived in Melbourne on a Wednesday afternoon. When I checked in, my boss said Friday would be my last day with the company (as well as the other three's last day). The reason for the sudden termination was that they had found a Middle Eastern agent with a fleet of aircraft like ours, which could support the F-15 program in Saudi Arabia. The fact that we had all left good jobs and made extensive arrangements and commitments meant nothing to the Harris Corp. They did this to their engineers "all the time." I said that future communications with me would be through my attorney. The others agreed that we would collectively sue Harris

Corp. for breach of contract. Lindsey Holland, nephew of the famous Florida senator Spessard Holland, was our attorney. He said that we had a good case because the Harris Corp.'s letter sent to me offering employment had the elements of a contract. The problem was that no one had been successful at suing Harris Corp. in their hometown of Melbourne before. The judges (most all of them) were firmly in the pockets of Harris Corp. So Harris' people tried to bully us into dropping the case. It took about three and a half years, but Harris finally asked to settle out of court. We all found better jobs. As far as I know, we were the only ones to have sued and won against Harris for breach of contract, even though they admitted to firing many engineers immediately after hiring them.

CHAPTER 9

New Orleans and West Palm Beach, Florida 1978 to 1984

After spending a few weeks on the beach in Melbourne, Florida, where we surf fished and negotiated with Harris Corp. through the lawyer, I found a nice chief pilot job with Tidewater Marine in New Orleans.

The CEO, John Laborde, and most of the staff were very southern—so much so that he would only hire a flight crew that was also from Dixie. I had to convince him that I was born and bred in the South. He was suspicious because of my accent, which had changed due to traveling and living in all parts of the world. I had a struggle getting him to accept my copilot, Bobby Bonham, who was from Kansas. Bobby wanted the job—his first jet job—so much that he virtually transformed himself into a very convincing southerner. He was not only an excellent pilot, but personable and efficient in everything. They loved Bobby. Tidewater Marine was a support company for offshore exploration activities. With over 400 ships, from crew boats to tugs, they mainly operated in the Gulf of Mexico, but also did some work in the Middle East, the North Sea, and other places.

One day in November, I was asked if I could fly four of the company leaders and attorneys to Oslo, Norway. I said sure, but the passengers might be more comfortable on a commercial airliner since we would have to stop for fuel several times in the Learjet 35. No, they said, the airline's schedules and connections would not get them there quickly enough. So I did some rapid flight planning and arrangements, and soon we were airborne on the way to Oslo, by way of Labrador, Iceland, and Scotland. Needless to say, it was snowing in Oslo when we approached. Everything—and I mean everything—was white and blended in with the snow. The frozen runway was plowed, but had been re-covered with snow since. I could only wonder how pilots could fly there all winter. We beat the Concorde's arrival by several hours, which made the passengers happy. The Concorde was a supersonic passenger jet with regular flights into Oslo in 1979. There had been a legal dispute over some ships that Tidewater had located in the North Sea, and the company was about to lose millions of dollars if they didn't show up and protect their interests. I found Oslo to be an interesting city with very kind people. We returned our passengers to New Orleans after a few days. I don't think their mission was too successful—foreign location, strange court procedures, et cetera. Anyway, it was another adventure, and for me, that's what it was all about. Tidewater also had other enterprises, such as land oil and gas operations, and a demolition company which was involved in the destruction of bridges and buildings.

We made several flights to Trinidad, where the company had boat operations. The "oil crunch" happened in the early 1980s and Tidewater support boats were not much in demand. They docked most of their ships by 1983, and there was some discussion about selling the plane. I started to look around for another operation.

I left Tidewater, and my copilot and I went to West Palm Beach, Florida, to work for John Rogers, a private investor who lived in a mansion on Palm Beach. Rogers promised that he intended to keep the aircraft indefinitely—but even at that time, he really planned to live on his sailboat, which he later had built. That meant the end of that job, when he sold the aircraft, a Learjet 35, to the factory. The factory then sold it to a company in Istanbul, Turkey.

During our first years in West Palm Beach, we lived in a home built in 1925. It was a very charming stucco with a two-story living room and classic early architecture of the Palm Beach area. After a time there, we realized that a "spirit" also was there. Several of our guests who stayed in a particular room would mention the following morning that something strange was in that room; a cold draft or just an uneasy feeling that something or someone was there. These reports came from different guests who did not know each other. Some were old, some young, but all had the same report. The dogs would never go into that room. Dottye had a teacher friend come to the house. When she went into that room, she said there was definitely a spirit and that she actually saw it. It seems that it was a middle-aged woman, dressed all in black. The lady in black did not seem hostile, other than strange occurrences with light bulbs flashing. That is, until we started talking about moving out, and that the house would probably be destroyed. Then we suddenly developed a terrible leak in the roof and an unusual drain blockage. About that time, we happened to speak to a passing stranger who was visiting our neighbor. The stranger said, "Oh, you live in the haunted house." After we sold the house to the airport, which bought most of the surrounding homes due to the noise from air traffic, Dottye and I locked the house for the last time and were walking down the driveway when Dottye was pushed from the back, causing her to fall forward to the ground. There was no one near us. Perhaps the lady was making a last point.

CHAPTER 10

Turkey Years

Through my contact at Learjet, I was put in touch with the Turks. The group in Istanbul was known as "Çukurova Holding." It was the second largest corporation in Turkey, owning large banks, insurance companies, automobile manufacturing plants, steel mills and a bottling company. The flights were mostly the chairman or his staff going to Western Europe, the Middle East, Russia and Kazakhstan, and other ex-Soviet countries.

When I first went to Istanbul, I made an agreement with Çukurova to create a new flight department, having only the one Learjet 35. It would be the first corporate flight department in Turkey, and what followed was one of the most painful, tedious, trying experiences of my life. This was made worse in that I did not speak Turkish, nor was I familiar with their customs. I quickly understood that words like "expedite," "right now," and "quick," although in their dictionary, were NEVER used, EVER. So, progress in arranging for private aircraft operations moved as quickly as a turtle mired in molasses. Tea was the ever-present ingredient at any meeting. Everyone we negotiated with assumed that without their sanction, we could not operate. The ultimate outcome was never in doubt, because the **Çukurova** chairman, Mr. Karamehmet was so powerful politically and economically. But the process remained unchanged because that's the way things had been done since the Ottomans were in control.

Then there was the job of hiring a mechanic and pilots. English was not an issue for the technician since you could just grunt and point to get the job done. Pilots were another matter. They have to at least manage "aviation English" to survive international flights. Most pilots there only spoke Turkish on the radio, which was OK if they did not leave Turkey. Turkish Airlines flew abroad, but the pilots were all happy with their jobs. After extensive searching, I located an ex-Turkish Navy pilot with a good command of English. He was egotistical and confrontational, but he was my only hope.

Dottye came to Istanbul, and we had a great stay at the Sheraton there. The food was very good, and we enjoyed the history and old structures in the city. We learned about the Ottomans and Kemal Ataturk, who in 1925 was responsible for changing Turkey from Islamic rule to a republic, which brought the country up to a point more equal with western Europe. Many Turks almost worshipped Ataturk; not as many do today, though. After about four months of writing manuals and standard operatinto a pointg procedures, and organizing the flight operations, we had to return to Florida when my mother had some health issues. I could not leave **Çukurova** with the one pilot, but I still had not located an English-speaking pilot. So I found a "rental pilot" in Germany, a reliable, Learjet-rated guy with perfect English, but the disposition of a Gestapo captain. Essentially, it was the "crew from hell"—safe, but far from pleasant. The Turks put up with this for a couple of years and before finally calling me, saying, "Captain, what would it take to get you to come back?" The situation had improved a lot with my mother and I could get away, so I made a contract with **Çukurova** that was sweet enough to make it worthwhile. This was the summer of 1988. They accepted my proposed contract, and in 1989 we left for Turkey with our three dogs, "Big Dog," "Little Dog," and "Puppy-Puppy."

The flight department had grown. Two helicopters had been added with two pilots. Also, three Learjet copilots were hired. And the same Turkish captain who I had originally hired before I left was still there. Had I been there, I would not have allowed most of these new pilots to be hired. The original captain, Savas, although intensely disliked by all of the other pilots, was still the only one who spoke English, could fly well, and could take flights when I could not. The Turks in our flight department were pretty intelligent, educated, and well behaved. But there remained a spark of Genghis Kahn that just wouldn't go away. Savas treated the other pilots like lower beings that had to be punished and demeaned constantly. Mostly the conflicts were verbal, but I did have to stop a physical encounter in which one of the pilots, after taking a verbal tirade from Savas, threw a desk chair at him. The chair, mercifully, only hit Savas a glancing blow in the head. I had to restrain the pilot who threw the chair to prevent him from a more lethal attack. I had to fire him, although I would have preferred to let Savas go, as he was the root cause of the flight department conflicts.

There were also maintenance technicians, cleaning crews, and a coordinator. We acquired more aircraft; the fleet grew to two Learjets, a Challenger, a King Air and two helicopters. The pilots could speak Turkish as long as the flights were within Turkey, and I was always flying the trips going abroad. We had many flights to the Middle East, Europe, Russia, Kazakhstan, and so on. We finally found an American pilot, who was a real blessing—smart, capable, and cooperative.

I had another issue with Savas. He had so antagonized the others that they refused to fly with him. I had a talk with the CEO of Çukurova, who said I could punish or demote Savas, but could not to fire him. So, I demoted him from the chief pilot position and replaced him with the American. This arrangement went pretty well, but Savas continued to cause problems.

We made a few trips in the Challenger to Kazakhstan, Uzbekistan, and other ex-Soviet countries. One of the things required for the flight back to Istanbul was to obtain catering or food for the passengers. The crew had to go to the food preparation facility to pick up the meals for the flight. It almost defies description: a combination of a meat-packing plant and the kitchen from hell. The smell is still rather vivid—not good at all! But the people there were very friendly and helpful. We raced across the ice-covered ramp in a dilapidated truck with the catering, which the passengers hardly touched.

On one such trip to Kazakhstan, where the boss was meeting with the president of the country, we waited six hours past our scheduled departure time. I had no way to contact the passengers, the weather in Istanbul was deteriorating, and our crew was tired and had little sleep since leaving Istanbul. The passengers showed up in the early hours of the morning. A night flight in icy conditions, with an exhausted crew and approaching weather minimums was just too much for me. I told the boss to go back, find a hotel, and wait for morning, when we could safely depart. I really thought that would be my last day on the job, but it wasn't. I don't regret the decision, and we lived to fly another day. I think most old pilots and safety-conscious passengers would understand.

Dottye and I got involved with a group called the American Research Institute in Turkey (ARIT), mostly associated with the consulate. The group went on some wonderful tours, such as China, and often Dottye joined them. I also joined them on a tour of western Turkey, which included places like Ephesus and several other historical sites. We traveled on a chartered bus and were having a great time when I was contacted by the flight department. They were requiring me to return ASAP for a trip with the Challenger, our large aircraft, to Kazakhstan. We arranged for them to send a helicopter to pick me up near the town where we were on the tour, but there was no airport or heliport there. I told them to pick me up four kilometers northwest on a certain road. The map I had did not exactly match the helicopter pilot's map. So he was looking for me on a different road a few kilometers away. I caught sight of him in the distance and went after him in a taxi. I left the taxi when we got as close as possible to the helicopter. The taxi driver helped with the bags and ran behind me across a plowed field to where the helicopter had just landed and was waiting for me. The flight back to Istanbul was about an hour. The Challenger was ready for departure with my copilot aboard and passengers on the way.

During these days in Turkey, Dottye went on a trip to China with ARIT. The trip included an expert on the region. It was a fantastic experience that included the Gobi Desert and a province in China that was predominately muslim. That province is known not only for its interesting history and customs, but for its separatist movement, which can provide substantial violence. There was no violent activity at the time Dottye was there, but, when she and I were in Zurich a few months later, we saw in a newspaper that the hotel where she stayed was partially destroyed by a separatist bomb. Too close for our taste!

The time we spent in Turkey was wonderful as we think back. It is a place with history going back thousands of years. We were surrounded by sultans' palaces, gigantic mosques, the old bazaar, the Golden Horn seaport, and the Bosporus. That channel divides Istanbul into two parts, part in Europe and part in Asia. The fish was excellent at the restaurants along the Bosporus, and you could get tasty doner kebab almost anywhere. The social life was enjoyable, as we had a big group of friends, both Turkish- and English-speaking. There was a huge party for us when we left.

In early 1994, the company let me know that I would be replaced by a Turkish captain since he could manage the flight department for a fraction of my contract cost. Economic conditions had indeed been more strained lately; the government had taken over two of the company's banks, and other financial problems were causing cash flow issues. So, we returned to West Palm Beach, where we had the same house we had been leasing since we left in 1989. We had to fix a lot of damage the tenant caused.

Our departure from Istanbul was a circus. Ten days before departure, one of our dogs had a puppy. She simply jumped onto the bed one night and gave birth. One of our rules is "No dog left behind," so the little one traveled in the cage with her mom, Peppino. That made it five dogs for Delta to fly to Dallas. The Cukurova flight department guys were wonderful, providing a passenger bus to take us all, including dogs, to the airport. They escorted us all to the gate, where Delta was ready to hustle the dogs down to the luggage area before the Turkish customs could check on them. You see, one of the dogs was a Kangal, which is

Turkey's national dog and is illegal to take out of Turkey. I was prepared to bribe the customs official, but didn't need to after all.

In preparation for leaving Turkey with four dogs and a puppy, Dottye filled an orange plastic trash can with dog toys, bones, and blankets. We then sealed it with tape so it wouldn't open and lose the contents. After the very stressful loading of the dogs, immigration, et cetera, we were relaxing in the gate area when an announcement said, "Would Mrs. Smith please come to the gate?" This couldn't be a good thing, we thought. We both approached the gate area to find the orange garbage can sitting alone on the counter. The customs official said, "What is in this container?" Dottye said, "Dog bones, toys, and blankets." The official said we should open it. When we opened the can, the official said, "Bones, toys, and blankets." We said, "Yes, we know." Our flight connected in Frankfurt, where we were waiting to depart for Dallas when the announcement came again, "Mr. or Mrs. Smith, please report to the customs area." We did, only to find the same orange garbage can, the same question about the contents, and the same request to open it. The agent looked at the items and said, "Dog bones, toys, and blankets." You would think this would be the end of the orange garbage can episode, but no. Once again, as we were processing through customs in Dallas with our many bags and belongings, we saw the infamous garbage can sitting all alone on one of the loading counters. The American customs agent had the same question about the can's contents and instructions for us to open it. The result was a replay of the previous two: "Dog bones, toys, and blankets." Amid all of this, we were concerned about some of the things we had packed in our bags that were antiques and perhaps would attract the attention of customs. But all of that was forgotten when the sound of a dog screaming filled the hallways and the ticketing areas of Dallas/Fort Worth Airport. That was our few-week-old puppy, Canim (pronounced "Jenum"), which means "my darling" in Turkish. No, we could have passed the Star of India through customs without so much as a question then, for all the airport officials wanted was to get that screaming dog out and gone!

The orange garbage can is still with us, full of dog food. The color is only slightly faded. Canim took over the pool, never missing a day swimming, and loved playing with the grandchildren when they were here. Baby, the special Turkish national dog, grew fast, and I took her to obedience training. There I met a lady who bred Kangals, also known as Anatolian Shepherds. She got us connected with a couple who owned a male Kangal and were willing to breed him. So the arrangements were made, and Baby had eight adorable pups. Well, we had the not-so-bright idea to start a kennel, selling some of the puppies for $1,200 each. We shipped dogs to Michigan, Tennessee, and California. We discovered the $1,200 did not cover the vet, food, and other costs, but it was an interesting experience. I gave one to our son Chip. That one grew to be a wonderful, 180-pound male. The Kangal has been the main dog in Turkey for over 3,000 years. Used for guarding sheep or cattle, they are kept in pairs for safety. The Turks cut their ears short and place a collar with spikes on their necks, making them invincible when attacking wolves.

We have always had dogs and the occasional cat. I believe we owe a lot to them. They have been as important to us as mortar to bricks in a house.

CHAPTER 11

The Return

We returned to the West Palm Beach house on Whippoorwill Trail in 1994, satisfied that we had a great five years in Istanbul. For the next four years, I worked as a charter pilot for a company in Naples, Florida, and also a company in Bridgeport, Connecticut. I did get an interesting job flying a Learjet for an English baron. This required that I fly the Learjet from Naples to Gloucestershire Airport in England. The contract provided that Dottye would come with me. We did very little actual flying while there. There was a problem finding a qualified copilot. But Dottye and I had a wonderful time exploring the Gloucestershire area of England. The baron and baroness were gracious and showed us around their mansion, which dated back to the 1200s. Dottye came with us on a flight to Nice, France. The baron and his wife were staying with friends in Monte Carlo, but the air conditioning had failed and they were quite uncomfortable. Our accommodations at a small hotel were pretty bad, so we moved to the Ramada at Monte Carlo, where we had a nice two or three days. A week or so after returning to England, the baron decided he would not need the plane, so we prepared to fly back to Naples. Trips across the North Atlantic in that Learjet, which did not have the latest GPS or other long-range navigation system, took me back to my first crossing in the B-47, using celestial navigation systems. I had bought a handheld GPS for this crossing since the air traffic control in Canada, Iceland, and Scotland were becoming more demanding of aircraft position accuracy.

The next few years were unremarkable compared to those from 1958, when we got married, until now. Not as many adventures or wild experiences as before. In 1998, I was employed as a simulator and ground instructor for Flight Safety International, where I was employed until 2018. I have to say it has been the best job yet. I was dedicated to it from the beginning, focusing on training pilots to be as good and as safe as possible, thus protecting them as well as their passengers. The clients were from Italy, Germany, Spain, Russia, China, South America, and the Middle East, as well as other places. Many became my close friends. The years I spent overseas served me well to communicate and understand their cultures—as well as their language, in some cases. The Flight Safety Team was fantastic. While there, I received the FAA Wright Brothers Master Pilot award for fifty years of flight, Pilot Instructor of the Year twice, and the Best of the Best in 2011. In 2016, I had a stroke, which partially disabled me for four to five months, but I returned to full duty in 2017. Later complications resulted in disability. But I can't complain. I lived a dream life, blessed by God, with a wonderful wife for sixty years, three great children, ten grandchildren, and a great-grandson, none of whom have divorced, committed crimes, or taken drugs. All of which are a miracle these days.

I have often said that I'm happy to have been born when I was. My grandfather had to deal with the Civil War, my father dealt with

Reconstruction, my children dealt with the Cold War, and my grandchildren are in the "social media generation." I used computers in my work, and they helped me get the job done. We can do things faster and more efficiently now, but we are paying a price for this. Life is much more impersonal. People don't trust each other and don't have the face-to-face interaction we once had. Lawyers fill great chunks of the phonebooks. Widespread paranoia exists. There is little trust, and that is sad. People turn to drugs because they can't cope with life as it is. Suicide is rampant. But there is something else that has happened in our country that continues to have a devastating and lasting effect. I call it the "National Conscience." Its result has been self-punishment of our society for the mistreatment of a people or race. The idea is good, but unfortunately it has been taken to the extreme, to the point of defeating the initial purpose. An example would be Affirmative Action, which in many cases led to the advancement of individuals solely due to their race, denying more qualified people advancement. Extreme movements render extreme results. What happened to "moderation in all things?" Our leadership in America has succumbed to influences that would like to forget that our country was created on Judeo-Christian principles. The truth is being ignored and an attempt made to modify history. It reminds me of documents subpoenaed from agencies that have so many deletions (classified information) that the complete meaning is lost. Robert E. Lee was at one time considered a great man and general, but now the National Conscience has determined him to be a criminal, thereby removing his statues and monuments. Some of the same generals and officers that opposed General Lee in the Civil War were responsible for the unforgivable mistreatment of Native Americans during the "Trail of Tears." Who should cast the first stone? The rewriting of history has made General Custer a hero and martyr instead of the self-glorifying killer that he was.

I'm an old man now. I'm not much for physical activity. I have no regrets about how I went through life. I was richly blessed.

When I do take my final flight, I hope I climb through the overcast sky and pop out on top of an endless deck of clouds to see God's glorious sunrise.

What an adventure!

Lee with client at flight simulator

WHERE RAINBOWS ARE

Lee Smith

The things I've done, the things I've tried;

Some for naught, some for pride;

Loved and lived while time would buy —

And found that rainbows start up high.

A thousand times, I cursed my lot,

Then turned to see just who had not;

Then tread my path along this beach,

That thread of light one time to reach.

With every slip, another try,

To find this aura formed so high;

Through distant hopes, with sordid fears,

And painful falls, a sea of tears,

Would only dim my upward scan

To find a place beyond this land.

I can't explain just how or why,

But rainbows start there in the sky.

Not for handheld gains my heart has cried,

But higher planes my soul to ride;

Would that I stretch the passing years

And fill my life beyond the mind.

And so my eyes once more will scan

And penetrate this hopeless land;

To times and spaces that seem to hide,
Then with a rainbow I collide.
And reaching here in dazzling splendor,
Understanding firm and clear,
Spread before me as a vision,
Space and time abruptly sheared.
Now with this cursory probe beyond,
I contemplate this bright new thought
With rationale of earthly mind,
And know so clearly this truth so bold:
That there are tears that leave the heart,
And other tears that serve the soul.
Each time reaching higher still,
Each point a test of strength and will;
I stand and raise my soul to God
With hope anew and courage filled,
To see with all my bursting might
And stretch the limits of my sight.
But once again—it's always there:
That cloud, that mist, to so impair
My gaze to things and worlds up high,
A rainbow there that passes by.
To give me promise through this maze;
To know in time that I'll know why
These rainbows start there in the sky.

Dottye and I with two of our grandchildren